The George Washington University
Washington, DC

Written by Julie Gordon

Edited by Kimberly Moore and Meryl Sustarsic

Layout by Jon Skindzier

*Additional contributions by Omid Gohari,
Christina Koshzow, Chris Mason, Joey Rahimi,
and Luke Skurman*

ISBN # 1-4274-0065-2
ISSN # 1551-0129
© Copyright 2006 College Prowler
All Rights Reserved
Printed in the U.S.A.
www.collegeprowler.com

Last updated 06/07/07

Special Thanks To: Babs Carryer, Andy Hannah, LaunchCyte, Tim O'Brien, Bob Sehlinger, Thomas Emerson, Andrew Skurman, Barbara Skurman, Bert Mann, Dave Lehman, Daniel Fayock, Chris Babyak, The Donald H. Jones Center for Entrepreneurship, Terry Slease, Jerry McGinnis, Bill Ecenberger, Idie McGinty, Kyle Russell, Jacque Zaremba, Larry Winderbaum, Roland Allen, Jon Reider, Team Evankovich, Lauren Varacalli, Abu Noaman, Mark Exler, Daniel Steinmeyer, Jared Cohon, Gabriela Oates, David Koegler, and Glen Meakem.

Bounce-Back Team: Alex Mizrahi, Stefanie Jackowitz, and Adina Matusow.

College Prowler®
5001 Baum Blvd.
Suite 750
Pittsburgh, PA 15213

Phone: 1-800-290-2682
Fax: 1-800-772-4972
E-mail: info@collegeprowler.com
Web Site: www.collegeprowler.com

How this all started...

When I was trying to find the perfect college, I used every resource that was available to me. I went online to visit school websites; I talked with my high school guidance counselor; I read book after book; I hired a private counselor. Sure, this was all very helpful, but nothing really told me what life was like at the schools I cared about. These sources weren't giving me enough information to be totally confident in my decision.

In all my research, there were only two ways to get the information I wanted.

The first was to physically visit the campuses and see if things were really how the brochures described them, but this was quite expensive and not always feasible. The second involved a missing ingredient: the students. Actually talking to a few students at those schools gave me a taste of the information that I needed so badly. The problem was that I wanted more but didn't have access to enough people.

In the end, I weighed my options and decided on a school that felt right and had a great academic reputation, but truth be told, the choice was still very much a crapshoot. I had done as much research as any other student, but was I 100 percent positive that I had picked the school of my dreams?

Absolutely not.

My dream in creating *College Prowler* was to build a resource that people can use with confidence. My own college search experience taught me the importance of gaining true insider insight; that's why the majority of this guide is composed of quotes from actual students. After all, shouldn't you hear about a school from the people who know it best?

I hope you enjoy reading this book as much as I've enjoyed putting it together. Tell me what you think when you get a chance. I'd love to hear your college selection stories.

Luke Skurman
CEO and Co-Founder
lukeskurman@collegeprowler.com

Welcome to College Prowler®

During the writing of College Prowler's guidebooks, we felt it was critical that our content was unbiased and unaffiliated with any college or university. We think it's important that our readers get honest information and a realistic impression of the student opinions on any campus—that's why if any aspect of a particular school is terrible, we (unlike a campus brochure) intend to publish it. While we do keep an eye out for the occasional extremist—the cheerleader or the cynic—we take pride in letting the students tell it like it is. We strive to create a book that's as representative as possible of each particular campus. Our books cover both the good and the bad, and whether the survey responses point to recurring trends or a variation in opinion, these sentiments are directly and proportionally expressed through our guides.

College Prowler guidebooks are in the hands of students throughout the entire process of their creation. Because you can't make student-written guides without the students, we have students at each campus who help write, randomly survey their peers, edit, layout, and perform accuracy checks on every book that we publish. From the very beginning, student writers gather the most up-to-date stats, facts, and inside information on their colleges. They fill each section with student quotes and summarize the findings in editorial reviews. In addition, each school receives a collection of letter grades (A through F) that reflect student opinion and help to represent contentment, prominence, or satisfaction for each of our 20 specific categories. Just as in grade school, the higher the mark the more content, more prominent, or more satisfied the students are with the particular category.

Once a book is written, additional students serve as editors and check for accuracy even more extensively. Our bounce-back team—a group of randomly selected students who have no involvement with the project—are asked to read over the material in order to help ensure that the book accurately expresses every aspect of the university and its students. This same process is applied to the 200-plus schools College Prowler currently covers. Each book is the result of endless student contributions, hundreds of pages of research and writing, and countless hours of hard work. All of this has led to the creation of a student information network that stretches across the nation to every school that we cover. It's no easy accomplishment, but it's the reason that our guides are such a great resource.

When reading our books and looking at our grades, keep in mind that every college is different and that the students who make up each school are not uniform—as a result, it is important to assess schools on a case-by-case basis. Because it's impossible to summarize an entire school with a single number or description, each book provides a dialogue, not a decision, that's made up of 20 different topics and hundreds of student quotes. In the end, we hope that this guide will serve as a valuable tool in your college selection process. Enjoy!

OMID GOHARI ◯ CHRISTINA KOSHZOW ◯ CHRIS MASON ◯ JOEY RAHIMI ◯ LUKE SKURMAN ◯
The College Prowler Team

Table of Contents

Introduction from the Author

When my parents first suggested that I look at colleges in Washington, DC, one image came to mind: gray-haired senators. Having only traveled to the District in middle school to visit national landmarks, I pegged it as an elderly, politically-driven city. But the minute I stepped onto GW's campus and saw thousands of students exploring their surroundings, I knew my preconceived notions about GW and Washington were totally false.

GW is a perfect school to attend if you're interested in politics—many students intern on Capitol Hill or at the White House, and political science is one of the most popular majors. Attending college in DC will increase your awareness of the political process and the world around you, but for those students whose interests lie in areas other than the government, there is also plenty to do and see.

GW is geared toward active, involved students who want to take advantage of city life and campus activities. Although GW admissions officials weigh applicants' grade point averages and class ranks heavily, they favor well-rounded students who made an impact in their high school communities. Most GW students do well in classes but could do better if they were not so busy with extracurricular activities. Academics at GW are pretty challenging, so be prepared to spend some quality time at the library, as well as on the field or stage, or at the podium.

Despite its location in the middle of Washington, DC, GW feels like it has a traditional campus because of its relatively small size and plethora of on-campus activities. The University is separate and distinct from the rest of the city and new buildings pop up on the ever-expanding campus almost every semester. In the past few years, the University built homes both for the Elliott School of International Affairs, and for the School of Media and Public Affairs. After a short delay involving legal issues with the city, GW began construction on a new building for the School of Business. The University also built and acquired state-of-the-art dorms and recently constructed a Greek Townhouse Row, among other projects.

The four years you spend in college will shape your life in ways you cannot imagine. If you are applying to schools, use this book to help you learn about GW and the great city of Washington, DC. If you've decided GW is the place for you, this book will help you explore the University and the District, which you will soon be able to call home.

Julie Gordon, Author
The George Washington University

By the Numbers

General Information

The George Washington University
2121 Eye St. NW
Washington, DC 20052

Control:
Private

Academic Calendar:
Semester

Religious Affiliation:
None

Founded:
1821

Web Site:
www.gwu.edu

Main Phone:
(202) 994-4949

Admissions:
(202) 994-6040

Student Body

**Full-Time
Undergraduates:**
9,797

**Part-Time
Undergraduates:**
1,170

**Total Male
Undergraduates:**
4,794

**Total Female
Undergraduates:**
6,173

Admissions

Overall Acceptance Rate:
38%

Early Decision Acceptance Rate:
63%

Regular Acceptance Rate:
36%

Total Applicants:
20,159

Total Acceptances:
7,726

Freshman Enrollment:
2,669

Yield (% of admitted students who actually enroll):
35%

Early Decision Available?
Yes

Early Action Available?
No

Early Decision One Deadline:
November 1 for Part One
December 1 for Part Two

Early Decision Two Deadline:
December 1 for Part One
January 15 for Part Two

Early Decision One Notification:
Mid-December

Early Decision Two Notification:
Early February

Regular Decision Deadline:
December 1 for Part One
January 15 for Part Two

Regular Decision Notification:
Late March

Must-Reply-By Date:
May 1

Applicants Placed on Waiting List:
2,284

Applicants Accepted from Waiting List:
788

Students Enrolled from Waiting List:
178

Transfer Applications Received:
2,109

Transfer Applications Accepted:
781

Transfer Students Enrolled:
351

Transfer Applicant Acceptance Rate:
37%

Common Application Accepted?
Yes

➜

Supplemental Forms?
Yes

Admissions E-mail:
gwadm@gwu.edu

Admissions Web Site:
http://www.gwu.edu/~go2gw

SAT I or ACT Required?
Either

**First-Year Students
Submitting SAT Scores:**
94%

**SAT I Range
(25th–75th Percentile):**
1180 – 1370

**SAT I Verbal Range
(25th–75th Percentile):**
590 – 690

**SAT I Math Range
(25th–75th Percentile):**
590 – 680

SAT II Requirements:
None

Retention Rate:
92%

**Top 10% of High
School Class:**
59%

Application Fee:
$60

Financial Information

Full-Time Tuition:
$34,030

Room and Board:
$10,470

Books and Supplies:
$850

**Average Need-Based
Financial Aid Package
(including loans,
work-study, grants,
and other sources):**
$30,891 per year

**Students Who Applied for
Financial Aid:**
52%

**Students Who Received
Financial Aid:**
39%

**Financial Aid Forms
Deadline:**
April 22

Financial Aid Phone:
(202) 994-6620

Financial Aid E-Mail:
finaid@gwu.edu

Financial Aid Web Site:
http://gwired.gwu.edu/finaid

Academics

The Lowdown On...
Academics

Degrees Awarded:
Bachelor
Master
Doctorate

Most Popular Majors:
28% Social Sciences
18% Business, Management, Marketing
8% Psychology
7% English Language and Literature
4% Computer Science

Undergraduate Schools:
Columbian College of Arts and Sciences
School of Business
School of Engineering and Applied Science
Elliott School of International Affairs
School of Media and Public Affairs
School of Medicine and Health Sciences
School of Public Health and Health Services

→

Full-time Faculty:
814

Faculty with Terminal Degree:
743

Student-to-Faculty Ratio:
13:1

Average Course Load:
5 classes per semester

Graduation Rates:
Four-Year: 72%
Five-Year: 78%
Six-Year: 79%

Best Places to Study:
Gelman Library 4th, 5th, and 6th floors
Kogan Plaza
The monuments
Barnes and Noble in Georgetown

Sample Academic Clubs:
American Islamic Medical Association
Biological Sciences Club
Finance and Investment Club
French Club
GW Academic Competition Club
GW World Literature Club
International Affairs Society
Philosophy Club

AP Test Score Requirements
Possible credit for scores of 4 or 5

IB Test Score Requirements
Possible credit for scores above 6

Special Degree Options

Seven-year Integrated BA/MD

Eight-year Integrated Engineering and Medicine Program

Integrated Engineering and Law Program

Five-Year Bachelor's/Master's programs: BA in Political Science/ Master of Public Policy

BA/MA in Women's Studies

BA or BS in Economics/Master of Public Policy

BA or BS in Computer Science/MS in Computer Science

BS/MA in Economics

BS/MS in Systems Engineering/Systems Engineering or Engineering Management

BS/MA in Systems Engineering/Economics

BS/MS in Economics/Systems Engineering or Engineering Management

BA/MA in Art or Psychology/Art Therapy

BS/MS in Chemistry/Forensic Sciences

BBA/MTA in Business Administration and Tourism Administration

BA/MPA in Criminal Justice and Public Administration

BBA/MSIST in Business Administration and Information Systems Technology

Did You Know?

GW has recently implemented a freshman writing course, University Writing 20. It focuses on **improving students' writing and researching skills**. Two-thirds of the freshman class is participating this year.

Don't think GW's library resources stack up to Georgetown's? GW students **have access to the nearby University's collection**, as well as to four other DC-area schools' resources. The six universities are part of the Washington Research Library Consortium, which allows member institutions' students to borrow materials from any of the libraries and have them delivered to their campus free of charge.

If you want to explore the city while getting academic credit, apply for an internship at a law firm, television network, or other organization. Most majors allow students to **receive up to six credits** for interning at a company or institution related to their field of study.

Although GW previously accepted academic credit from more than 2,000 study abroad programs, the University **stopped taking transfer credit** from programs not affiliated with the University in fall 2003. The list of accepted options now includes about 200 programs.

Students Speak Out On...
Academics

"The professors are generally good. You really need to research the professors for the classes you want to take. You will find a lot of professors with amazing experiences, but others won't have so much."

Q "The teachers are pretty nice. They are all accessible. And although **some have unfair grading practices**, all in all, I can't really complain. Professors are recognized experts in their respective fields. Current and former ambassadors, as well as presidential advisers often teach here."

Q "Teachers vary—as a freshman, you will be in a lot of large, impersonal classes, but as you move into upper-level courses, they get better. **Professors are very knowledgeable in their subject matter**. They are accessible to answer your questions during their office hours, and they are especially good with e-mail."

Q "I don't think academics at GW are much harder than high school. I do the bare minimum for most of my classes and still have a 3.9 grade point average. You learn that for some classes or professors **you really need to do all of the reading** and assignments, but for others you really don't have to do anything—not even show up for class. It all depends on the professor and how interested you are in the class."

Q "The required courses are pretty boring, but the classes I have to choose from are really interesting. **The teachers are hit or miss**. I tend to get a lot of professors with very thick accents, which makes learning harder."

Q "**Being a smaller, private school means students receive closer attention**. This can work to your disadvantage, because in some classes, you can't disappear—the teacher will most likely know you."

Q "The professors are knowledgeable, and for the most part, they are passionate about their areas of study. But I have found **only a few who are able to inspire** that zeal in their students. The classes are only as interesting as the professors themselves."

Q "**Professors are extremely accessible**; they always complain that students do not utilize their office hours enough. I have found nearly every professor I've had to be very reasonable and willing to help. Getting into the classes you want is also not difficult. GW has a writing center where you can go and get your papers proofread, edited, or even outlined and organized. As long as you're not doing your paper the night before, it's a very helpful service."

Q "I'm an English major, so classes are pretty specific, and I don't have any teaching assistants, which is mostly a positive thing. For the larger introductory classes, I think it's fine, in concept, to have TAs teach discussions while professors teach lectures, but the TAs here are often too timid, and they're just learning the material while the students are. But I think that becomes less of a problem after the first level of courses. **I think the academics at GW are good**, and the classes are mostly interesting. It depends what you take."

Q "Most classes are very interesting and stimulating. In the international affairs program, **a lot of professors have experience in the field** and/or currently work for the government. Most professors are easy to reach outside of class and willing to help with anything you need."

Q "I love my major and my classes. The School of Media and Public Affairs provides very interesting and helpful classes that will come in handy in my future career. But **the school needs to offer more classes per semester** and more teachers to teach them."

Q "Although not as personal as in high school, **teachers are genuinely interested in helping students** understand subject material."

The College Prowler Take On...
Academics

Although introductory lecture classes are often dull and cover basic topics, most students say they benefit from their upper-level classes. GW requires freshmen to take a significant number of General Curriculum Requirements (GCRs), so history majors may have to suffer through "Baby Bio," and pre-med students may be forced to plow through art history. But a talented professor can make any class interesting. Most intro classes are taught by a professor twice a week, lecture-style. Then a teaching assistant leads a discussion or lab once a week. Because they are graduate students, some TAs seem too consumed with their own research to care much about students, while others are more helpful than the professors. Most undergrads agree that as they move into more specialized classes, professors are more engaged in the subject matter and more experienced in their fields.

And this goes for the higher-profile professors, as well—the University's location in the heart of Washington allows for top experts in every field to teach a course or two at GW. Well-known professors in every school and many departments—including the School of Media and Public Affairs's Steve Roberts, *Washington Post* writer and *ABC News* anchor Cokie Roberts's husband—may have students on waiting lists for more than a year, and even that doesn't guarantee a spot. Students' crusades to get into certain classes prove that a professor has a great deal of influence on the enjoyment and academic worth of a class.

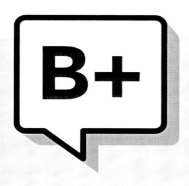

The College Prowler® Grade on

A high Academics grade generally indicates that professors are knowledgeable, accessible, and genuinely interested in their students' welfare. Other determining factors include class size, how well professors communicate, and whether or not classes are engaging.

Local Atmosphere

The Lowdown On...
Local Atmosphere

Region:
Mid-Atlantic

City, State:
Washington, DC

Setting:
Major city

Distance from Baltimore:
1 hour

Distance from Philadelphia:
3 hours

Distance from New York:
5 hours

Points of Interest:
Dupont Circle
National Mall
National Monuments
National Zoo
Smithsonian Institute Museums

➜

Closest Movie Theaters:

AMC Courthouse Plaza
2150 Clarendon Blvd.,
Arlington, VA
(703) 998-4AMC

AMC Union Station
50 Massachusetts Ave. N.E.,
Northeast
(703) 998-4AMC

Dupont Circle 5
1350 19th St. NW,
Dupont Circle
(202) 872-9555

Major Sports Teams:

Capitals (hockey)
Nationals (baseball)
Redskins (football)
Wizards (basketball)

Closest Shopping Malls:

Pentagon City Mall
The Shops at Georgetown Park
Tyson Corner Center

City Web Sites

www.dc.gov
www.dc.org
www.dc.about.com

Did You Know?
5 Fun Facts about DC:

- Students can attend the presidential inauguration at the White House every four years. Those interested can either stand in the general admissions area or get **free "gold" tickets**—which allow for closer access than general admissions tickets—by calling their state representatives.

- DC's **National Cherry Blossom Festival** attracts hundreds of thousands of spectators each spring. The 9,000 trees lining the Tidal Basin were a gift to the District from Japan in 1912.

- GW and DC have been involved in a five-year-long conflict concerning the University's expansion into the surrounding area. Neighbors claim that **GW is taking over quiet Foggy Bottom**, but GW tried arguing in court that disallowing expansion would violate the DC Human Rights Act, which prohibits discrimination based on matriculation, among other categories. District Court disagreed, but extended the University's deadline for coming into compliance with DC zoning requirements.

- District residents are **fighting to get representation** in the Senate and House of Representatives. Although those living in DC are taxed, they receive no representation other than a non-voting delegate because they do not technically live in a state.

- Of **adults age 25 and older** in the District, 42 percent hold at least a bachelor's degree.

Famous People from DC:

Carl Bernstein

Duke Ellington

Al Gore

Goldie Hawn

Ben Stein

Local Slang:

The Hill – Capitol Hill, where several GW students intern

The Mall – Not a place to go shopping, the National Mall is home to a variety of monuments and museums

The Metro – Washington's subway system

Students Speak Out On...
Local Atmosphere

"The only place I would avoid is Southeast DC. It's a very poor neighborhood, and there is some gang violence there. Not to worry, though, because GW is located far from it in Northwest DC."

"DC is a great place to go to school. It's certainly a city, but in a very real sense, it has the qualities of an intimate town. It's the most unique gathering of people and ideas I've ever experienced. Some parts of the city are sketchier than others, so make sure you know where you're going when you get on the Metro. **You'll never run out of stuff to visit**."

"I would recommend visiting all the Smithsonian museums, which are free of charge and a really nice experience. If you have nothing to do, you could always **walk down to the monuments at night**—it's really beautiful, and something you wouldn't have the opportunity to do elsewhere. Also, if you get an internship, which most students do, you'll have a great opportunity to explore another aspect of the city."

"**DC is amazing**. There are lots of college kids and other young professionals in town. There is so much to do and so many opportunities, but you definitely have to make an effort in order to benefit from such opportunities. Some people think DC is really dangerous, just being in the city and with terrorism concerns, but if you are careful and smart, it's not a problem."

Q "There are tons of things to do in DC—take in a show at the Kennedy Center, party, go for monument walks, see museums, visit historical sites, listen to different political speakers. **The atmosphere is very political**, obviously."

Q "**Georgetown and American universities are the two closest schools around**, although I rarely visit them. As for DC, my biggest regret is not taking advantage of everything it has to offer. The list of things to do is way too long. Don't limit yourself, but don't make yourself crazy. Common street smarts are helpful. Don't be completely oblivious to things, such as hanging around Southeast, also known as 'the ghetto,' at 2 a.m."

Q "After Boston, DC is the largest college town. There are too many places that are worth seeing to list, but some of the best include the monuments, museums, Embassy Row, and Adams Morgan. **You should have little reason to stray into areas you should not visit**, such as Northeast DC."

Q "**DC is very eclectic**. There are people from all different backgrounds, ethnicities, religions, and socio-economic situations. There are lots of colleges and young professionals in the area, and since Congress changes every four years, there are always new people coming in."

Q "DC is a great city. American and Georgetown are two other major universities, and there are some smaller ones, as well. DC is quieter than New York or Boston, yet there is always something to do or see. **Museums and government sites can get old rather quickly**, but there are always new exhibits and events coming through DC."

Q "DC has everything to offer. Georgetown is really close, and you'll probably hang out there eventually. In Maryland, they have the University of Maryland College Park, which is Metro-accessible. **If you're looking for a big state party school, that's where to go**. I hang out there a lot, and they have lots of raging parties!"

The College Prowler Take On...
Local Atmosphere

GW's location in the Foggy Bottom area of DC gives it a unique flavor with which no other university can compare. With government officials working nearby, the school often seems to blend into the city, but GW's five-by-six block radius definitely feels like a traditional college campus. The University's close proximity to bars, clubs, museums, national monuments, sports arenas, and theaters exposes students to the entire cultural experience that is DC. Students call the city an "amazing place," and most can't imagine living for four years in a rural environment after spending a day in DC.

At most college campuses, students hang out on their universities' quads in between classes. Although GW students often toss around Frisbees during the spring and summer, they are also out and about in the District, constantly exploring new things. People interested in the arts can see a Broadway show on tour at the National or Warner Theaters, or go to one of the several movie theaters near campus, which show both commercial flicks and independent films. Sports fans can take a quick train ride to Baltimore to cheer on the Orioles or catch a Wizards game at the MCI Center, which is also a major concert venue. Another perk of living so close to the monuments are the beautiful nighttime views—there is nothing like watching a breath-taking meteor shower while lying beside the reflecting pool, and you can't spend four years at GW without hooking up at the monuments (your forefathers would be proud).

The College Prowler® Grade on

A high Local Atmosphere grade indicates that the area surrounding campus is safe and scenic. Other factors include nearby attractions, proximity to other schools, and the town's attitude toward students.

Safety & Security

The Lowdown On...
Safety & Security

Number of GW Police Officers:
95

Phone:
(202) 994-6111 (emergencies)

(202) 994-6110
(non-emergencies)

Safety Services:
4-RIDE escort van

Colonial Express shuttle bus

Blue-light emergency phones

Free taxi service to the Mount Vernon campus

Rape Aggression Defense Systems classes

Health Services:
Emergency Medical Response Group on-call 24 hours a day

GW Hospital on campus

Student Health Services on campus

Health Center Office Hours:
Monday–Wednesday
8:30 a.m.–6:30 p.m.,
Thursday–Friday
8:30 a.m.–4:30 p.m.,
Saturday 9 a.m.–12:30 p.m.

Did You Know?

GW often hires **outside security officials** and forbids non-GW community members from entering residence halls during major protests near campus.

Several men's bathrooms on GW's campus are listed as **"hotspots" for sexual activity** on the Web site *www.cruisingforsex.com.* The University Police Department (UPD) has periodically participated in undercover bathroom sting operations since the department discovered lewd activity in the bathrooms in November 1999.

GW hired an assistant vice president for emergency safety management in response to the **September 11th attacks**.

The University has a **four-level alert system**, separate from the national system.

Metropolitan Police arrested nine GW students in spring 2004 who were **protesting unfair work practices** in the Marvin Center. The charges were dropped.

The UPD recently received an additional $180,000 to **buy more 4-RIDE escort vans**, hire additional drivers, and create another shuttle bus route.

Students Speak Out On...
Safety & Security

"Well, considering there was a girl mugged outside her building on a Tuesday night at 8 p.m., I would say that the campus needs to be more concerned with individual safety and less with underage drinking."

Q "I feel very safe at GW. In addition to the District's Metropolitan Police Department (MPD), GW has its own University Police Department (UPD). In the evenings, GW operates a van escort service that will pick you up and drive you to wherever you need to go within three city blocks of campus. In addition, **there is a shuttle service that has various stops throughout the campus** that runs approximately every 10 minutes throughout the night."

Q "**I feel very safe on campus**. In all the freshman dorms, there are cameras everywhere. There are security guards at the desk to make sure that only GW students and their signed-in guests are entering the dorm. I would say that, all in all, the campus is pretty safe, with some isolated instances of crime. I would not advise walking alone at night, but the campus provides minivan and shuttle transportation to and from all campus locations during the night. The area where GW is located, Foggy Bottom, is one of the nicer and safer areas of DC."

Q "Security is so tight there that it eventually gets annoying. You need to swipe your student ID everywhere you go and have friends sign in when they visit. UPD can take you from place to place in a car after dark so you don't have to walk alone. **Safety is not an issue at GW**."

Q "Because the campus is in a city, security is a big issue. In the freshman dorms and the student center, a security guard is on duty at all times. However, in other GW buildings, security is lacking. There once was an incident when a man entered one of the upperclassman dorms without passing any security and had access to students' rooms. The security officials at **GW then blamed it on the students who let the man into the building**, since there was no one guarding the door and UPD thought the students should've been more careful about who they 'let' walk in the door. GW officials didn't feel as though they were at fault. I think that the school is totally to blame for not having a guard at the front entrance."

Q "GW is pretty great with safety and security. It's in the business district of DC, so after about five or six in the evening, it gets pretty empty except for students. It's a really close-knit campus, except for a few dorms that are a little bit farther out—the Aston, Hall on Virginia Avenue, and City Hall. UPD is located at the center of campus, and they patrol after dark and walk the halls of dorms. **To enter the dorms, you have to use your GWorld student ID**, and you're required to sign guests in. UPD takes its job pretty seriously. There have been a few incidents this year, but I've felt safe all year long."

Q "Since we are located so close to many government buildings, **we have a mix of MPD and Secret Service constantly on campus**. During the day, I always feel safe, and at night, I usually take the University-provided 4-RIDE service wherever I need to go. UPD is decent, as well, and the University takes safety very seriously."

Q "**I can honestly say that I feel safe on campus**. I often walk around at night alone. However, there have been incidents of robberies and violence at GW. We live right in a city, so it's something to think about. You definitely need to have street smarts."

The College Prowler Take On...
Safety & Security

The University places great emphasis on security and safety. The security presence on campus is three-fold, with University Police, Metropolitan Police, and the Secret Service constantly monitoring the area. There is a UPD force that patrols the campus 24-hours-a-day by foot and van. GW also has a 4-RIDE escort van service, which operates from 7 p.m. until 6 a.m. daily. Students can call 4-RIDE when they want a ride from one point on campus to another, and a van will also take students up to about three blocks off-campus. The only complaint about the service—and it's a big one—is that 4-RIDE is very slow. Students may wait for a van for up to an hour or so on a Saturday night. GW makes a good effort in trying to keep its students safe, but even with all the precautions, crime occurs. The larger freshman dorms have the best security on campus—each has a "three-swipe system." Residents must first swipe their GWorld ID cards outside the dorm before entering, then in front of a UPD officer at the desk, and finally at the stairwells and elevators. Visitors must be signed into the building. This may seem like unnecessary measures, but it makes students feel secure.

After all, the campus is located in the middle of Washington, which has one of the highest crime rates in the country. Within the past few years, some students have even been held at gunpoint. However, most students will never encounter even a petty crime firsthand while on GW's campus. Foggy Bottom is a safe neighborhood compared to the rest of the city; nevertheless, being in the nation's capital, problems do arise. Overall, GW makes an effort, and the majority of students feel secure on campus.

The College Prowler® Grade on

A high grade in Safety & Security means that students generally feel safe, campus police are visible, blue-light phones and escort services are readily available, and safety precautions are not overly necessary.

Computers

The Lowdown On...
Computers

High-Speed Network?
Yes

Wireless Network?
On some parts of campus

Number of Labs:
13, plus labs in most
residence halls

**Number of Computers
in Labs:**
580

Operating Systems:
PC, Mac

→

24-Hour Labs:

Rome Hall B1, B104, T205

Phillips Hall T306

Monroe Hall 102B

Funger Hall 636

Eckles Library 142, 113

Marvin Center G04

Most residence hall labs

Charge to Print?

Yes, nine cents per page in all campus computer labs, excluding those in residence halls.

Did You Know?

GW **struck a deal with Napster** in the summer of 2004 to provide free access after students were charged with illegal downloading. Response to the service has been overwhelmingly negative.

Each student receives an **Ethernet** (high-speed Internet connection) in his or her dorm room.

Each student gets an **"@gwu.edu" e-mail address** upon entering GW, which expires a few months after graduation. Although alumni for the past few years have been able to keep their GW e-mail addresses indefinitely, the University cut the privilege in the academic year and gave alumni forwarding "@alumni.gwu.edu" addresses instead.

The University is currently working to **expand wireless access** to the student center, called the Marvin Center, and several classroom facilities. The business school building, which is currently under construction, will be completely wireless.

Students Speak Out On...
Computers

"I would strongly recommend bringing your own computer. Labs are numerous but often become crowded during the day. The convenience of having your own computer cannot be overstated."

Q "GW has 24-hour computer labs all over campus and in most residence halls. For the most part, they use Dell computers, but there is a Mac lab, as well. The computer labs are not always crowded, but they do seem to fill up during finals. I would recommend bringing your own computer. **The residence halls are wired for Ethernet**, so that's very convenient, as well."

Q "**The computer labs aren't always crowded**, but they are not that dependable, especially with the printers. They usually run out of ink or paper, and it takes a while for the office to figure that out—the school is run like a business and is one major bureaucracy. I would suggest bringing a computer and a printer if you can. If not, you could probably mooch off of a friend."

Q "Computer labs can get crowded during cram periods of the semester, but you can always try another lab. **The dorm computer labs are never full**, but sometimes they are not as high-tech as the main computer labs. I would only recommend bringing your own computer if you need to personalize your settings or if you are on it 22 out of the 24 hours of the day like I am."

Q "Bringing a computer is very helpful—most people do. However, you can live without one. **Computer labs are available 24 hours a day**, which makes it fairly easy to get a computer at some point during the day. Also, your roommates and friends will probably have computers that they will let you use."

Q "The computer network is usually good, although in the school year, there were some **serious problems with the e-mail system**. Computer labs in the library and the Marvin Center are usually crowded, but there are other less crowded labs around campus."

Q "You should seriously consider having a computer of your own. **You rarely have a written assignment that you are not required to type**. Computer labs, in my experience, are usually crowded, but I've never had to wait a really long time to get access to a computer. Sometimes classes are held in there, such as Chemistry 003 and 004 Labs."

Q "**Computer services on campus aren't that great**. If you want to get your computer fixed or need help installing programs, you have to look off campus or to other students who know how to fix computers."

The College Prowler Take On...
Computers

And the survey says, "Bring your own computer to school!" Although GW has several computer labs in convenient locations such as the Marvin Center and most dorms, the majority of students say they cannot live without their personal computers. Students must type all of their papers and assignments, which is easier to do from a dorm room than a crowded computer lab. Most students also want a computer for personal reasons. Everyone at GW is constantly on AOL Instant Messenger, which makes keeping in touch with friends convenient. Since all dorm rooms are capable of Ethernet connection, it makes sense to bring a computer to school.

For those students who cannot bring a computer to school, GW's labs, located all over campus, are adequate. However, the labs can get really crowded about a half an hour before classes begin, and it is almost impossible to get a computer during exam time. In May 2004, GW increased the printing fee from seven to nine cents per page in all University computer labs excluding those in residence halls, so it is wise to purchase a printer if you plan on printing a lot of documents. Although the University is trying to expand its wireless network, a complete classroom conversion will not happen for years, if ever. GW's labs are just fine, but are often crowded, and computers sometimes break. That and the printing fee, which could increase even more in the future, make personal computers a worthwhile investment.

The College Prowler® Grade on

A high grade in Computers designates that computer labs are available, the computer network is easily accessible, and the campus' computing technology is up-to-date.

Facilities

The Lowdown On...
Facilities

Student Center:
The Marvin Center

Campus Size:
43 acres

Athletic Centers:
The Lerner Health and
Wellness Center
The Smith Center

Popular Places to Chill:
Kogan Plaza
J Street
In front of the Marvin Center
The Hippodrome

Libraries:
5

What Is There to Do on Campus?

Although GW is located directly in the heart of Washington, on-campus activities add to the feeling of campus unity. Students can enjoy free movie screenings and plays put on by student production companies and the Department of Theatre and Dance. Between classes, most students hang out on Kogan Plaza, one of two outdoor, grassy areas, or in J Street, the student center's dining and seating area. GW basketball games are fun, and the men's team did well in the 2004–05 season with its first NCAA Tournament appearance in six years, so many students attended games. There are also comedy shows, cultural festivals and celebrations, and countless other activities every week on campus.

Movie Theater on Campus?

No, but student organizations often sponsor free movies on the University Quad or in the Marvin Center.

Bowling on Campus?

Yes, located on the Marvin Center's fifth floor, the Hippodrome.

Bar on Campus?

Yes, The University Club.

Coffeehouse on Campus?

Yes, Starbucks in the Marvin Center and Gelman Library.

Favorite Things to Do

In the warmer months, Fall Fest and Spring Fling are student favorites. Put on by the student-run Program Board, the two events are a day's worth of concerts, games, and free food. Although the festivals have attracted rap artists for the past couple of years, about which some students complain, other on-campus concerts offer a variety of music. No Doubt, John Mayer, Counting Crows, and Guster have also performed at the Smith Center, where GW basketball games are played. Up-and-coming acts often play in the Marvin Center or at other venues around campus. Kogan Plaza also hosts musical acts and other outdoor activities.

Students love barbecuing and sun tanning in Kogan during the very hot DC summers. A farmers' market—a relatively new event—also takes place in Kogan every few months, allowing vendors from around the city to sell baked goods, fresh fruit, jewelry, and artwork. Besides Kogan, most students love hanging out with friends in J Street, the food court in the Marvin Center. Starbucks is a great spot to meet a study group, since the library is always crowded, and the "library police" flip out if you try to sneak in a vanilla latte.

Students Speak Out On...
Facilities

"Facilities are top-of-the-line at GW. I just wish they would put more money into academics and less into building new facilities."

Q "GW is a wealthy school that **puts a lot of money back into the campus**. Computers are updated every few years. The school recently opened a gym facility called the Lerner Health and Wellness Center. The student center is also great—it has offices for student organizations, a bookstore, food court, bowling alley, and pool hall."

Q "One of the best things about GW is that it is constantly building new facilities for the students, and they are always beautiful. **Several years ago, the University built a state-of-the-art gym with basketball courts**, a track, squash courts, and workout rooms. It also recently built a new location for the School of Media and Public Affairs (SMPA) and finished a new International Affairs building. The student center is very modern and clean."

Q "GW prides itself on its facilities. **All the buildings are constantly redone, rebuilt, and maintained**. You'll be very impressed if you see the campus. GW recently completed a building for its SMPA, which is the permanent home of CNN's *Crossfire*."

Q "There is a great Health and Wellness Center that is free for students to use. Well, you pay for it in your tuition. It's awesome. The student center is the Marvin Center where there are tables to sit around and floors upstairs that have student club rooms and bowling. **We also have some plazas and areas where you can sit outside**."

Q "**I absolutely love the campus facilities**. The student center is the best I've seen on any other campus, the main computer centers are all of the newest quality, and the athletic facilities are accessible to everyone. But if you are on a sports team, traveling to the Mount Vernon campus for the main fields can be a hassle if you don't live there."

Q "The Health and Wellness Center weight room is really small. **There's no large pool for lap swimming**. There's no big outdoor track, and the Center is small—but it is a nice facility. The soccer/lacrosse field on the Mount Vernon campus is beautiful, and club teams even get to use it."

Q "Facilities are pretty nice. In fact, I would say they're too nice. This is a flaw—our **University spends too much money on image and not enough on functionality**."

Q "I go to the gym five days a week, and the Health and Wellness Center is amazing. I love it, and **it has everything you could possibly want**. The student center is okay. It has what you need, but it is nothing special. They are always building stuff all around campus to expand."

Q "GW has some of the best facilities I have ever seen on a college campus. The Marvin Center, which is the student center, is great. **Everything's pretty convenient**."

Q "Facilities are generally really good, and almost everything is new or has been recently upgraded. **Classroom shortages have been a problem**, but they recently finished the Elliott School's new building."

The College Prowler Take On...
Facilities

GW students have always griped that the University spends too much money on facilities and goes overboard when renovating or building new structures—the infamous "Gold Pillar" in the Marvin Center is a perfect example of the University's extravagance—but no one complains when using brand new equipment in these multimillion-dollar structures. In the past few years, GW built homes for the School of Media and Public Affairs and the Elliott School of International Affairs, which cost about $100 million altogether. The campus also recently built a fantastic gym, the Lerner Health and Wellness Center, dubbed the "Hell Well" by students. It has cardiovascular machines, a weight room, racquetball courts, and a swimming pool. Despite an adequate number of machines, the lines can be quite lengthy during peak times.

Overall, students are pleased with GW's facilities. The only facilities on campus in poor condition are certain classrooms. Rooms in the Academic Center, where several classes are held, are rather rundown, with small desks and wobbly chairs. Corcoran Hall, home to the Science Departments and laboratories, has outdated and inadequate laboratories and equipment, and University officials have said they would like to renovate the building. The newer buildings, however, are gorgeous; each time the University builds a new facility, it's top-of-the-line and pleasing to the eye.

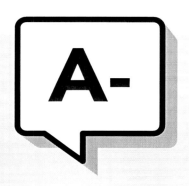

The College Prowler® Grade on

A high Facilities grade indicates that the campus is aesthetically pleasing and well-maintained; facilities are state-of-the-art, and libraries are exceptional. Other determining factors include the quality of both athletic and student centers and an abundance of things to do on campus.

Campus Dining

The Lowdown On...
Campus Dining

Freshman Meal Plan Requirement?

Yes

Meal Plan Average Cost:

$1,050 per semester

$1,500 minimum per semester for freshmen

Places to Grab a Bite with Your Meal Plan:

Ames Dining Hall

Food: Buffet-style

Location: Mount Vernon Campus

Favorite Dish: Pancakes

Hours: Monday–Friday 11 a.m.–2 p.m. (lunch), Saturday–Sunday 11 a.m.–2 p.m. (brunch), Monday–Sunday 5 p.m.–8 p.m. (dinner)

Bene Pizza

Food: Pizza

Location: J Street Food Court

Favorite Dish: Individual barbecue chicken pizza

Hours: Monday–Friday 11 a.m.–8 p.m.

Big Burger

Food: Hamburgers, sandwiches, French fries

Location: The Hippodrome (fifth floor of the Marvin Center)

Favorite Dish: Big Burger and fries

Hours: Monday–Wednesday 11:30 a.m.–11 p.m., Thursday–Friday 11:30 a.m.–2 a.m., Saturday–Sunday 5 p.m.–11 p.m.

Burger King Expressway

Food: Hamburgers, sandwiches

Location: J Street Food Court

Favorite Dish: Whopper

Hours: Monday–Thursday 7:30 a.m.–10 a.m. (breakfast), Monday–Thursday and Sunday 11 a.m.–10 p.m., Friday–Saturday 11:30 a.m.–10 p.m.

Chick-fil-A Express

Food: Chicken sandwiches, chicken nuggets, salads

Location: J Street Food Court

Favorite Dish: Chicken nuggets and French fries

Hours: Monday–Saturday 11:30 a.m.–9 p.m.

Colonial Express

Food: "Grab and Go" Sandwiches and Salads

Location: Marvin Center Ground Floor

Favorite Dish: Soup and salad

Hours: Monday–Sunday 8:30 a.m.–8 p.m.

Crepeaway

Food: Crepes

Location: J Street Food Court

Favorite Dish: Banana, chocolate and whipped cream in a crepe

Hours: Monday-Friday 10 a.m.–8 p.m.

Einstein Bros. Bagels

Food: Bagels, muffins, soups, salads

Location: Marvin Center Ground Floor

Favorite Dish: Tasty Turkey on a sesame bagel

Hours: Monday–Friday 8 a.m.–6 p.m., Saturday–Sunday 9 a.m.–4 p.m.

Funger Express

Food: "Grab and Go"

Location: Funger Hall

Favorite Dish: Mozzarella and tomato sandwich

Hours: Monday–Thursday 7:45 a.m.–4 p.m.

The Home Zone

Food: Home-cooked meals, pasta, omelets (breakfast only)

Location: J Street Food Court

Favorite Dish: Rotisserie-style chicken, create-your-own pasta

Hours: Monday–Friday 7 a.m.–8 a.m. (breakfast), Sunday 10 a.m.–9 p.m., Monday, Tuesday, Thursday noon–9 p.m., Wednesday 12 p.m.–2 p.m. (lunch)

Jamba Juice

Food: Fruit smoothies

Location: Marvin Center Ground Floor

Favorite Dish: Raspberry smoothie

Hours: Monday–Thursday 8:30 a.m.–9 p.m., Friday 8:30 a.m.–8 p.m., Saturday–Sunday noon–6 p.m.

Kaz Sushi Bistro

Food: Japanese

Location: J Street Food Court

Favorite Dish: California roll and edamame

Hours: Monday–Thursday 11:30 a.m.–8 p.m., Friday 11:30 a.m.–4 p.m.

Montague's Deli

Food: Sandwiches, salads, soups

Location: Marvin Center Ground Floor

Favorite Dish: Grilled panini

Hours: Sunday–Thursday 11 a.m.–9 p.m.,

(Montague's Deli, continued)

Friday–Saturday 11:30 a.m.– 7 p.m.

The Noodle Bar

Food: Chinese

Location: J Street Food Court

Favorite Dish: Chicken with Chinese vegetables

Hours: Monday–Friday 11:30 a.m.–8 p.m.

Pan Geo Wraps

Food: Wraps

Location: J Street Food Court

Favorite Dish: Chicken caesar wrap

Hours: Monday–Thursday 11:30 a.m.–8 p.m., Friday 11:30 a.m.–2 p.m.

Provisions Market

Food: Supermarket

Location: Marvin Center Ground Floor

Favorite Dish: Milk and cereal

Hours: Sunday–Thursday 8 a.m.–12 a.m., Friday– Saturday 10 a.m.–9 p.m.

Provisions Market Too

Food: Gourmet supermarket

Location: Marvin Center Ground Floor

Favorite Dish: Fresh cheese

Hours: Monday–Friday 10 a.m.–8 p.m., Saturday–Sunday 10 a.m.–6 p.m.

The Pub and Convenience Store at Mount Vernon

Food: Grill, supermarket

Location: Mount Vernon campus

Favorite Dish: Hamburger and French fries

Hours: Monday–Thursday 7:30 a.m.–11 p.m. (grill closes at 10 p.m.), Friday–Saturday 8:30 a.m.–9 p.m., Sunday 8 a.m.–11 p.m. (grill opens at 1 p.m.)

Salad Works

Food: Salads

Location: J Street Food Court

Favorite Dish: Create-your-own salad

Hours: Sunday–Thursday 11 a.m.–9 p.m., Friday–Saturday 11:30 a.m.–7 p.m.

Starbucks

Food: Coffee, Pastries

Location: J Street Food Court

Favorite Drink: Caramel Frappucino

Hours: Monday–Thursday 7 a.m.–12 a.m., Friday 7 a.m.–11 p.m., Saturday 8 a.m.–11 p.m., Sunday 8 a.m.–12 a.m.

Subway

Food: Sandwiches

Location: J Street Food Court

Favorite Dish: Teriyaki chicken sandwich

Hours: Sunday–Thursday 11:30 a.m.–12 a.m., Friday–Saturday 11:30 a.m.–11 p.m.

Taco Bell Express

Food: Mexican

Location: J Street Food Court

Favorite Dish: Soft taco

Hours: Monday–Sunday 11:30 a.m.–12 a.m.

Thurston Dining Hall

Food: Buffet-style, "Grab and Go"

Location: Thurston Hall

Favorite Dish: Sandwich

Hours: Monday–Friday 7:30 a.m.–10 a.m. (breakfast) and 11 a.m.–2:30 p.m. (lunch), Saturday–Sunday 11 a.m.–2:30 p.m. (brunch), Monday–Sunday 5 p.m.–8 p.m. (dinner)

→

Off-Campus Places to Use Your Meal Plan:

Armand's Pizza
1140 19th St. NW,
Foggy Bottom
(202) 331-9500

Aroma Indian Cuisine
1919 Eye St. NW,
Foggy Bottom
(202) 833-4700

Au Bon Pain
2000 Pennsylvania Ave. NW,
Foggy Bottom
(202) 887-9215

Bertucci's Brick Oven Pizzeria
2000 Pennsylvania Ave. NW,
Foggy Bottom
(202) 296-2600

The Burro
2000 Pennsylvania Ave. NW,
Foggy Bottom
(202) 293-9449

Campussnacks.com
(202) 337-0567

Capitol Grounds
2100 Pennsylvania Ave. NW,
Foggy Bottom
(202) 293-2057

Cluck-U-Chicken
2921 Georgia Ave. NW,
(202) 726-0006

Cone E Island
2000 Pennsylvania Ave. NW,
Foggy Bottom
(202) 822-8460

DJ's Fastbreak
22nd and G streets NW,
Foggy Bottom
(202) 429-0230

Domino's Pizza
2029 K St. NW,
Foggy Bottom
(202) 223-1100
3255 Prospect St. NW,
Georgetown
(202) 342-0100

Espresso and More
H Street, in front of the
Gelman Library

Froggy Bottom Pub
2142 Pennsylvania Ave. NW,
Foggy Bottom
(202) 338-3000

Haagen Dazs
3120 M St. NW,
Georgetown
(202) 333-3443

H Street Underground
2300 H St. NW,
The Hillel
(202) 994-5090

Hunan Peking
3251 Prospect St. NW,
Georgetown
(202) 337-8888

La Prima
2000 Pennsylvania Ave. NW,
Foggy Bottom
(202) 887-1001

The Little Café
3314 M St. NW,
Georgetown
(202) 333-7677

Malaysia Kopitiam
1827 M St. NW,
Georgetown
(202) 833.6232

Manny and Olga's
1641 Wisconsin Ave. NW,
Georgetown
(202) 337-1000

Mehran Restaurant
2138 Pennsylvania Ave. NW,
Foggy Bottom
(202) 342-0056

Olympia
3207 O St. NW,
Georgetown
(202) 338-2478

One Fish Two Fish
2423 Pennsylvania Ave. NW,
Georgetown
(202) 822-0977

Panda Café
2138 Pennsylvania Ave. NW,
Georgetown
(202) 337-3366

Papa John's Pizza
2525 Pennsylvania Ave. NW,
Georgetown
(202) 293-7272

Philadelphia Cheesesteak Co.
3347 M St. NW,
Georgetown
(202) 333-8040

Philadelphia Pizza
1201 34th St. NW,
Georgetown
(202) 333-0100

Pizza Italia
1917 F St. NW,
Foggy Bottom
(202) 589-0898

Quick Pita
1210 Potomac St. NW,
Georgetown
(202) 338-PITA

Sizzling Express
538 23rd St. NW,
Foggy Bottom
(202) 659-1234

Subway
2033 K St. NW, Foggy Bottom
(202) 833-1363

T.G.I. Friday's
2100 Pennsylvania Ave. NW,
Foggy Bottom
(202) 872-4344

Thai Place Restaurant
2134 Pennsylvania Ave. NW,
Foggy Bottom
(202) 298-8204

Zero's Subs
1015 20th St. NW,
Foggy Bottom
(202) 785-1500

Student Favorites:

Au Bon Pain
Bertucci's
Chick-fil-A
Cone E Island
Einstein Bros. Bagels
Froggy Bottom Pub
Hunan Peking
Little Café
Papa John's Pizza
Pizza Italia
Sizzling Express
T.G.I. Friday's
Thai Place

Other Options

One of GW's greatest traditions lies in a small cart parked near
the Marvin Center. Manouch, a hot dog vendor, sells his delicious
franks and hot pretzels late into the night after most other dining
venues are closed. There's nothing like a Manouch dog to satisfy
the late-night munchies after an evening of partying. There are
also a few snack carts near the Gelman Library and a vendor near
Kogan Plaza who sells coffee, cappuccino, and pastries. Students
must pay cash at most carts; only the Espresso and More cart
accepts the GW meal plan.

Did You Know?

GW recently introduced a new dining plan called **Colonial Cash**. Students can eat at participating on- and off-campus dining venues and restaurants using meal plan points at each. GW does not operate on a "meals per week" system. Colonial Cash is a declining balance system, meaning students can spend their dining points wherever they want, whenever they want. Whether students want to spend all their points on Domino's pizzas or go grocery shopping at Provisions to do their own cooking, Colonial Cash allows for it.

The Colonial Cash system also works at some non-food venues, such as **the GW Bookstore**, CVS, and Esteem Cleaners.

Some on-campus dining venues welcome a "**Visiting Chef Series**" once a week. Visiting chefs are from local restaurants and cook their best dishes. Students can use their meal plan to pay.

Students Speak Out On...
Campus Dining

"Food on campus is pretty good, but GW is in the middle of a major city, so you can eat about any food you can imagine just by walking a few blocks or jumping on the Metro."

"**Food is delicious on campus**. GW operates on a meal plan system by which, rather than paying per meal, you pay for whatever you eat. The main eatery on campus is called J Street, which is a food court-style dining facility. Downstairs is a supermarket and a gourmet market. In addition, some freshman residence halls have their own eating facilities."

"They really try to give students lots of food options at GW. Because there are tons of spots around GW's campus to grab a sandwich or a bagel, they are constantly changing the menus. At the student center, there are pasta, wraps, and sandwich stations, as well as Burger King, Chick-fil-A, Taco Bell, and Einstein Bros. Bagels. **My favorite meal is grabbing a pre-made gourmet sandwich from the supermarket downstairs** at the student center. I could get anything from mozzarella and tomato to chicken pesto. The dining halls at GW are only located in the freshman dorms. Sometimes they have visiting chefs come in and cook dinners, but other than that, they aren't that good."

"Food's okay. I am not a huge fast food fan, and we have a lot of that, but **there's a ton of options because we are in DC**. I think anyone would get sick of school food options over time. Each room has a microwave and fridge, and by sophomore year, you are likely to have a kitchen in your room."

Q "The food on campus is good, but probably like most college dining options, **you get sick of the choices**. Still, GW tries to accommodate all kinds of preferences, and the quality of the food is good. J Street is usually good, and having a small supermarket (Provisions) on campus lets us buy basically anything we need with dining points."

Q "Mount Vernon's Pub is a good change if you live on the main Foggy Bottom campus, and the **Marvin Center has a variety of food to eat**."

Q "As a freshman, you can survive eating campus food for the majority of the year. But for upperclassmen, Chipotle on F Street is a cheap yet tasty break, **the shops at 2000 Penn have some good restaurants**, and going to the special Tuesday meals on the Mount Vernon Campus are worth the trip. On special Tuesdays, lobster, steak, and assorted visiting chef meals can be served."

Q "Food on campus is generally pretty good. The University is making efforts to **keep places open later and give students more variety**. There are also many small restaurants and shops right near campus. La Prima and Au Bon Pain are great places to have lunch, and they take Colonial Cash."

Q "Food is okay. There are several options, and they continue expanding. However, it is still typical college food. The food court has lots of options, but they are not four-star restaurants; **they're fast food joints where the employees are union workers** and use that fact to take advantage of their jobs and not work very hard."

The College Prowler Take On...
Campus Dining

Although some universities work on a "meals per week" plan, GW's system is a little different and much more convenient. At the beginning of the semester, freshmen and others living on campus must purchase a meal plan, which works as a declining debit card. For example, if a student gets the $1,500-per-semester plan, he has $1,500 to spend at any on- or off-campus venue that accepts the GW Colonial Cash meal plan. Some non-food items can also be purchased. Extra points are carried over from the fall semester to the spring semester, but not from the spring to fall. Students like the convenience of GW's meal plan—no one tells them what to eat or when to eat it, and the variety of options is decent. J Street, the large food court in the Marvin Center, offers sushi, pizza, pasta, Chick-fil-A, Burger King, Taco Bell, and more. But many students quickly tire of these greasy fast food restaurants and wish the more popular venues—Subway and the pasta and salad stations—would vary what they offer.

Another common complaint concerning on-campus dining is that students get sick of their choices; there aren't enough healthy or vegetarian options. With the advent of Colonial Cash in the 2003-04 academic year, however, students can now choose from many different places. An additional bonus is that Colonial Cash exempts students from DC's 10 percent sales tax at on-campus locations. Even without that extra charge, though, food on and off campus is pricey. Nevertheless, the ease and convenience of GW's meal plan is a perk most students really enjoy.

The College Prowler® Grade on

Our grade on Campus Dining addresses the quality of both school-owned dining halls and independent on-campus restaurants as well as the price, availability, and variety of food.

Off-Campus Dining

The Lowdown On...
Off-Campus Dining

Restaurant Prowler:
Popular Places to Eat!

Anna Maria's
Food: Italian
1737 Connecticut Ave. NW, Dupont Circle
(202) 667-1444
Price: $30 and under per person
Hours: Monday–Thursday
11 a.m.–1 a.m.,
Friday 11 a.m.–3 a.m.,
Saturday 5 p.m.–3 a.m.,
Sunday 5 p.m.–1 a.m.

Bangkok Bistro
Food: Thai
3251 Prospect St. NW, Georgetown
(202) 337-2424
Price: $17 and under per person
Hours: Monday–Thursday
11:30 a.m.–10:45 p.m., Friday
11:30 a.m.–11:45 p.m.,
Saturday 12 p.m.–11:45 p.m.,
Sunday 12 p.m.–10:45 p.m.

→

Café Milano

Food: Italian

3251 Prospect St. NW,
Georgetown

(202) 333-6183

Cool Features: Outdoor
dining, late–night menu

Price: $36 and under
per person

Hours: Monday–Tuesday,
11:30 a.m.–1 a.m.,
Wednesday–Saturday
11:30 a.m.–2 a.m.,
Sunday 11:30 a.m.–11 p.m.

Café Japone

Food: Japanese

2032 P St. NW,
Dupont Circle

(202) 223-1573

Cool Feature: Karaoke

Price: $15 and under
per person

Hours: Monday–Sunday
5:30 p.m.–1 a.m.

Charlie Chiang's

Food: Chinese

1912 Eye St. NW,
Foggy Bottom

(202) 293-6000

Price: $15 and under
per person

Hours: Monday–Sunday
11 a.m.–10:30 p.m.

Chipotle

Food: Mexican

1629 Connecticut Ave NW,
Dupont Circle

(Chipotle, continued)

(202) 387-8261

Cool Feature: Dress up like a
burrito on Halloween and eat
one for free

Price: $9 and under
per person

Hours: Monday–Sunday
11 a.m.–10 p.m.

The Cheesecake Factory

Food: Variety

5345 Wisconsin Ave., NW,
Friendship Heights

(202) 364–0500

Price: $25 and under
per person

Hours: Monday-Thursday
11:30 a.m.–11:30 p.m.,
Friday–Saturday 11:30
a.m.–12:30 a.m., Sunday
10 a.m.–11 a.m.

Clyde's

Food: American, seafood

3236 M St. NW, Georgetown

(202) 333-9180

Price: $16 and under
per person

Hours: Monday–Thursday
11:30 a.m.–2 a.m., Friday
11:30 a.m.–3 a.m., Saturday
10 a.m.–3 a.m., Sunday
9 a.m.–2 a.m.

Cosí

Food: Sandwiches, salads,
desserts

1647 20th St. NW,
Dupont Circle

(Cosí, continued)

(202) 332-6364

Cool Features: Outdoor dining at some locations, make–your–own s'mores

Price: $8 and under per person

Hours: Monday–Thursday 7 a.m.–12 a.m., Friday 7 a.m.–1 a.m., Saturday 7:30 a.m.–1 a.m., Sunday 7:30 a.m.–12 a.m.

The Diner

Food: Sandwiches, breakfast

2453 18th St. NW, Adams Morgan

(202) 232-8800

Price: $10 and under per person

Hours: Monday–Sunday 24 hours

J. Paul's

Food: American

3218 M St. NW, Georgetown

(202) 333-3450

Price: $22.95 and under per person

Hours: Monday–Thursday 11:30 a.m.–2 a.m., Friday–Saturday 11:30 a.m.–3 a.m., Sunday 10:30 a.m.–2 a.m.

Jaleo

Food: Spanish (tapas, wines)

480 7th Street, NW, Downtown

(202) 628–7949

(Jaleo, continued)

Cool Feature: Award–winning head chef

Price: $30 and under per person

Hours: Monday 11:30 a.m.–10 p.m., Tuesday–Thursday 11:30 a.m.–11:30 p.m., Friday–Saturday 11:30 a.m.–12 a.m., Sunday 11:30 a.m.–10 p.m.

Kramerbooks and Afterwords Café and Grill

1517 Connecticut Ave. NW, Dupont Circle

(202) 387-1400

Cool Features: Café and bookstore, great brunch

Price: $17 and under per person

Hours: Monday–Thursday and Sunday 7:30 a.m.–1 a.m., Friday–Saturday 24 hours

Lauriol Plaza

Food: Mexican

1835 18th St. NW, Adams Morgan

(202) 387-0035

Cool Features: Outdoor dining, great margaritas and happy hour

Price: $17 and under per person

Hours: Monday–Thursday 11 a.m.–11 p.m., Friday–Saturday 11 a.m.–12 a.m., Sunday 11 a.m.–11 p.m.

Lindy's Red Lion

Food: Burgers, sandwiches

2040 I St. NW,
Foggy Bottom

(202) 785–2766

Cool Feature: Offers
outdoor dining

Price: $15 and under
per person

Hours: Monday–Friday 8
a.m.–9 p.m., Saturday–
Sunday
11 a.m.–9 p.m.

Old Ebbitt Grill

Food: American

675 15th St. NW,
Downtown

(202) 347–4800

Cool Feature: Senators often
spotted dining

Price: $30 and under
per person

Hours: Monday–Friday
7:30 a.m.–1 a.m., Saturday–
Sunday 8:30 a.m.–1 a.m.

Paolo's

Food: Italian

1303 Wisconsin Ave. NW,
Georgetown

(202) 333–7353

Cool Feature: Offers
outdoor dining

Price: $25 and under
per person

Hours: Sunday–Thursday
11:30 a.m.–11:30 p.m.,
Friday–Saturday 11:30 a.m.–
1 a.m.

Sequoia

Food: Pasta, seafood

3000 K St. NW,
Washington Harbour

(202) 944–4200

Cool Feature: Beautiful view
of the Potomac River

Price: $25 and under
per person

Hours: Monday–Saturday
11:30 a.m.–11:30 p.m.,
Sunday 10:30 a.m.–
10:30 p.m.

Singapore Bistro

Food: Assorted Asian

1134 19th St. NW,
Dupont Circle

(202) 466–1100

Cool Feature: 89–cent sushi

Price: $15 and under
per person

Hours: Monday–Thursday
11:30 a.m.–10:30 p.m.,
Friday 11:30 a.m.–11 p.m.,
Saturday 12 p.m.–11 p.m.,
Sunday 4 p.m.–10 p.m.

Smith & Wollensky

Food: Steak, seafood

1112 19th St. NW,
Dupont Circle

(202) 466–1100

Cool Feature: Offers
outdoor dining

Price: $60 and under
per person

Hours: Monday–Friday
11:30 a.m.–11:30 p.m.,
Saturday–Sunday 5:00
p.m.–11:30 p.m.

T.G.I.Friday's
Food: American

2100 Pennsylvania Ave., NW,
Foggy Bottom

(202) 872–4344

Price: $20 and under
per person

Hours: Daily, 11 a.m.–10 p.m

Tony and Joe's Restaurant
Food: Seafood

3000 K St. NW,
Washington Harbour

(202) 944–4545

Cool Features: Beautiful view
of the Potomac River, popular
spot for happy hour

Price: $32 and under
per person

Hours: Monday–Sunday
11 a.m.–10 p.m. (food),
11 a.m.–1:30 a.m. (bar)

Student Favorites:
Bangkok Bistro, Café Milano,
Chipotle, Lauriol Plaza, Lindy's
Red Lion, Old Ebbitt Grill

24–Hour Eating:
Kramerbooks and Afterwords
(on Fridays and Saturdays),
the Diner

Closest Grocery Stores:
Safeway

2550 Virginia Ave. NW,
Foggy Bottom

(202) 338–3628

(Closest Grocery Stores, continued)
Fresh Fields

2323 Wisconsin Ave. NW,
Georgetown

(202) 333–5393

Dean and Deluca

3276 M St. NW,
Georgetown

(202) 342–2500

Best Pizza:
Pizza Italia

Armand's

Best Chinese:
Hunan Peking

Best Breakfast:
The Diner, Kramerbooks
and Afterwords

Best Wings:
Old Ebbitt Grill

Best Healthy:
Cosí

Best Place to Take Your Parents:
Café Milano

Smith and Wollensky

Tony and Joe's

Students Speak Out On...
Off-Campus Dining

"There are cheap restaurants and really expensive ones, all of which are really good. I always go to Froggy Bottom Pub, Au Bon Pain, Bertucci's, Singapore Bistro, and a bunch of places in Georgetown."

Q "Being in a city, there are plenty of places to go, but be careful because a lot of them are expensive. DC could use some more cute places like Cosí instead of just having a billion Cosís on every block. Also good are Chipotle and the Cheesecake Factory, although Cheesecake is kind of far away in Friendship Heights. Kramerbooks and Afterwords in Dupont is fun, and my friends and I like J. Paul's in Georgetown. If you don't have somewhere in mind, **just go into G-town and you'll find something**, no problem."

Q "There are plenty of places to eat off campus when you get sick of the Marvin Center. Georgetown, Dupont Circle, and Adams Morgan all have a lot of good places. The Diner in Adams Morgan is a favorite of mine. However, **it gets pricey to eat out a lot**."

Q "The restaurants are good. **Georgetown is really close by**, within walking distance, and there are many good places to eat there. Also, being in a city, you will have millions of places to choose from that will suit your mood."

Q "DC is known for fine dining; **there are innumerable excellent establishments** within walking distance of campus. Try the Old Ebbitt Grill."

Q "The off-campus restaurants are amazing. Georgetown and Dupont Circle are extremely close and offer **loads of options**."

Q "Restaurants are decent. There's a T.G.I. Friday's, some small burger joints, and a Bertucci's right near campus. Within DC, **you can find any cuisine you might desire**."

Q "Restaurants are fantastic—it's DC! **Lindy's Red Lion is the local favorite**, but there are thousands of great restaurants in DC. Check out Anna Maria's, on Connecticut Avenue between R and S streets—for amazing Italian food and great service."

Q "Georgetown restaurants are always a close option, as well as downtown DC. More specifically, I enjoy Jaleo as a favorite Spanish restaurant, and **Chinatown has Dim Sum afternoons**."

The College Prowler Take On...
Off-Campus Dining

In the area surrounding GW's campus, there are several convenient and casual restaurants such as Chipotle, Cosi, and Lindy's Red Lion. There are also dozens of places that accept Colonial Cash. Many different kinds of tasty food can be found at restaurants in Georgetown and Dupont Circle—Filomena, in Georgetown, offers homemade pastas and other delicious Italian food; Levante's is great for Middle Eastern cuisine; the Daily Grill on Connecticut Avenue offers fresh meats, fish, and pastas; and Penang, in Dupont, serves delicious Malaysian cuisine. Georgetown offers an eclectic mix of American, Chinese, French, Indian, Vietnamese, and other cuisine. A fun place for late-night weekend eats is Kramerbooks and Afterwords, a 24-hour coffee shop and bookstore that serves desserts as well as entrees late into the night. Other than K&A, however, late-night eating options are definitely lacking on and around campus.

Washington's restaurant scene only adds to GW's exceptional local atmosphere. For students without a meal plan, outside restaurants are just as convenient to eat at as on-campus venues. Most students who live off-campus go out to lunch and dinner or order in pretty regularly, while those who are on a meal plan usually eat at restaurants where they can use their meal plan during the week, and then venture to off-campus restaurants that don't accept the meal plan during the weekend. Restaurants may be expensive, but with so many choices, everyone is sure to find a local favorite.

The College Prowler® Grade on

A high Off-Campus Dining grade implies that off-campus restaurants are affordable, accessible, and worth visiting. Other factors include the variety of cuisine and the availability of alternative options (vegetarian, vegan, Kosher, etc.).

Campus Housing

The Lowdown On...
Campus Housing

Room Types:
Singles, Doubles, Triples, Quads, Five-person and Six-person Suites

Best Dorms:
1959 E Street
City Hall
Ivory Tower
New Hall

Worst Dorms:
Crawford Hall
The Schenley
The West End

Undergrads Living on Campus:
63%

Number of Dormitories:
29

→

Dormitories:

1959 E Street
Floors: 10
Total Occupancy: 190
Bathrooms: In-room
Coed: Yes
Percent of Men/Women: 34%/66%
Percent of First-Year Students: 0%
Room Types: Single, double, triple, quad, five-person suites, one six-person suite
Special Features: Computer lab, kitchen in room, study lounge, washer and dryer in room

2109 F Street
Floors: 4
Occupancy: 70
Bathrooms: In-room
Coed: Yes
Percent of Men/Women: 39%/61%
Percent of First-Year Students: 0%
Room Types: Double, super double
Special Features: Computer lab, kitchen in room, laundry facilities

The Aston
Floors: 10
Total Occupancy: 222
Bathrooms: In-room
Coed: Yes
Percent of Men/Women: 38%/62%
Percent of First-Year Students: 0%
Room Types: Double
Special Features: Computer lab, kitchen in room, laundry facilities

Building JJ
Floors: 3
Occupancy: 19
Bathrooms: Shared
Coed: Yes
Percent of Men/Women: 64%/37%
Percent of First-Year Students: 0%
Room Types: Singles, one-bedroom apartments, two-bedroom apartments
Special Features: Kitchen in room, laundry facilities, TV lounge

City Hall
Floors: 12
Total Occupancy: 525
Bathrooms: In-room
Coed: Yes
Percent of Men/Women: 37%/63%

➜

(City Hall, continued)

Percent of First-Year Students: 0%

Room Types: Double, triple, super triple

Special Features: Computer lab, kitchen in room, laundry facilities, fitness room, meeting rooms, outdoor pool, study lounge

Clark Hall, on the Mount Vernon Campus

Floors: 3

Total Occupancy: 35

Bathrooms: Shared

Coed: No

Percent of Men/Women: 0%/100%

Percent of First-Year Students: 97%

Room Types: Double

Special Features: Computer lab, community kitchen, laundry facilities, TV lounge

Cole Hall, on the Mount Vernon Campus

Floors: 4

Total Occupancy: 38

Bathrooms: Shared

Coed: Yes

Percent of Men/Women: N/A

Percent of First-Year Students: 100%

Room Types: Double

Special Features: Computer lab, community kitchen, laundry facilities, TV lounge

Crawford Hall

Floors: 8

Total Occupancy: 157

Bathrooms: In-room

Coed: Yes

Percent of Men/Women: 38%/62%

Percent of First-Year Students: 0%

Room Types: Double, quad

Special Features: Computer lab, community kitchen, laundry facilities, TV lounge

The Dakota

Floors: 10

Total Occupancy: 210

Bathrooms: In-room

Coed: Yes

Percent of Men/Women: 55%/45%

Percent of First-Year Students: 1%

Special Features: Computer lab, kitchen in room, washer and dryer in room (except first floor), study lounge

Francis Scott Key Hall

Floors: 8

Total Occupancy: 153

Bathrooms: In-room

Coed: Yes

Percent of Men/Women: 26%/64%

Percent of First-Year Students: 0%

Room Types: Single, double, triple

➜

(Francis Scott Key Hall, continued)

Special Features: Computer lab, kitchen in room, laundry facilities, TV lounge, bicycle room, billiard room

Fulbright Hall

Floors: 8

Total Occupancy: 207

Bathrooms: In-room

Coed: Yes

Percent of Men/Women: 47%/53%

Percent of First-Year Students: 100%

Room Types: Triple, quad

Special Features: Computer lab, kitchen in room, laundry facilities, study lounge, TV lounge

Guthridge Hall

Floors: 8

Total Occupancy: 139

Bathrooms: In-room

Coed: Yes

Percent of Men/Women: 43%/53%

Percent of First-Year Students: 5%

Room Types: Single, double, triple

Special Features: Computer lab, kitchen or cooking equipment in room, laundry facilities, TV lounge

Hall on Virginia Avenue

Floors: 8

Total Occupancy: 461

Bathrooms: In-room

Coed: Yes

Percent of Men/Women: 43%/57%

Percent of First-Year Students: 97%

Room Types: Double, triple

Special Features: Computer lab, community kitchen in basement, laundry facilities, dining hall, fitness center, rooftop pool with deck, study lounge, TV lounge

Hensley Hall, on the Mount Vernon Campus

Floors: 3

Total Occupancy: 37

Bathrooms: Shared

Coed: No

Percent of Men/Women: 0%/100%

Percent of First-Year Students: 97%

Room Types: Double

Special Features: Computer lab, community kitchen, laundry facilities, TV lounge

International House

Floors: 9

Total Occupancy: 135

Bathrooms: In-room

Coed: Yes

(International House, continued)

Percent of Men/Women: 42%/58%

Percent of First-Year Students: 0%

Room Types: Single, double

Special Features: Computer lab, kitchen or cooking equipment in room, laundry facilities, bicycle room, billiards and ping-pong tables, rooftop deck, TV lounge

Ivory Tower

Floors: 10

Total Occupancy: 729

Bathrooms: In-room

Coed: Yes

Percent of Men/Women: N/A

Percent of First-Year Students: 0%

Room Types: Double, quad

Special Features: Five eating venues, several music rooms, underground parking garage, washer and dryer in room

Jacqueline Bouvier Kennedy Onassis Hall

Floors: 8

Total Occupancy: 246

Bathrooms: In-room

Coed: Yes

Percent of Men/Women: 34%/64%

Percent of First-Year Students: 0%

Room Types: Single, double, triple

(Jacqueline Bouvier Kennedy Onassis Hall, continued)

Special Features: Computer lab, kitchen in room, laundry facilities, TV lounge

Lafayette Hall

Floors: 8

Total Occupancy: 164

Bathrooms: In-room

Coed: Yes

Percent of Men/Women: 53%/47%

Percent of First-Year Students: 92%

Room Types: Double, triple

Special Features: Cooking facilities, laundry facilities, TV lounge, houses honors students and three Living and Learning Communities for first-year students (International Affairs, Politics and Values, and Roots of Western Civilization)

Madison Hall

Floors: 8

Total Occupancy: 187

Bathrooms: In-room

Coed: Yes

Percent of Men/Women: 30%/70%

Percent of First-Year Students: 0%

Room Types: Double, quad

Special Features: Computer lab, cooking facilities, laundry facilities, TV lounge

Merriweather Hall, on the Mount Vernon Campus

Floors: 3

Total Occupancy: 42

Bathrooms: In-room

Coed: No

Percent of Men/Women: 0%/100%

Percent of First-Year Students: 100%

Room Types: Single, double

Special Features: Computer lab, communal kitchen, laundry facilities, Student Health Services clinic, TV lounge

Mitchell Hall

Floors: 8

Total Occupancy: 349

Bathrooms: Shared

Coed: Yes

Percent of Men/Women: 49%/51%

Percent of First-Year Students: 34%

Room Types: Single

Special Features: Computer lab, community kitchen, laundry facilities, bicycle room

Munson Hall

Floors: 8

Total Occupancy: 147

Bathrooms: In-room

Coed: Yes

Percent of Men/Women: 43%/57%

Percent of First-Year Students: 0%

(Munson Hall, continued)

Room Types: Double, triple

Special Features: Computer lab, kitchen in room, laundry facilities, TV lounge

New Hall

Floors: 9

Total Occupancy: 430

Bathrooms: In-room

Coed: Yes

Percent of Men/Women: 38%/62%

Percent of First-Year Students: 0%

Room Types: Double, quad

Special Features: Computer lab, kitchen in room, laundry facilities, billiard room, TV lounge

Pelham Hall, on the Mount Vernon Campus

Floors: 3

Total Occupancy: 84

Bathrooms: Shared

Coed: Yes

Percent of Men/Women: 51%/49%

Percent of First-Year Students: 100%

Room Types: Single, double

Special Features: Balconies in most rooms, computer lab, community kitchen, laundry facilities, skylights in some rooms, TV lounge, community kitchen

The Schenley

Floors: 8

Total Occupancy: 142

Bathrooms: In-room

Coed: Yes

Percent of Men/Women: 34%/66%

Percent of First-Year Students: 0%

Room Types: Double, triple

Special Features: Computer lab, kitchen in room, laundry facilities, study lounge

Somers Hall, on the Mount Vernon Campus

Floors: 4

Total Occupancy: 246

Bathrooms: In-room

Coed: Yes

Percent of Men/Women: N/A

Percent of First-Year Students: 100%

Room Types: Single, double

Special Features: Computer lab, community kitchen, laundry facilities, fitness room, study lounge, TV lounge

Strong Hall

Floors: 6

Total Occupancy: 109

Bathrooms: Shared

Coed: No

Percent of Men/Women: 0%/100%

Percent of First-Year Students: 40%

Room Types: Single, double

(Strong Hall, continued)

Special Features: Computer lab, cooking facilities, laundry facilities, rooftop deck

Thurston Hall

Floors: 9

Total Occupancy: 1,051

Bathrooms: In-room

Coed: Yes

Percent of Men/Women: 41%/59%

Percent of First-Year Students: 100%

Room Types: Double, triple, quad, five-person suites, six-person suites

Special Features: Computer lab, dining hall, laundry facilities, fitness room, study lounge, TV lounge

The West End

Floors: 8

Total Occupancy: 171

Bathrooms: In-room

Coed: Yes

Percent of Men/Women: 40%/60%

Room Types: Double, triple, quad

Special Features: Kitchen in room, laundry facilities

Housing Offered:

Singles: 8%

Doubles: 37%

Triples/ Suites: 18%

Apartments: 33%

Other: 4%

Room Types
Residence hall-style
Students share one to three rooms, depending on the number of residents. The majority of rooms have a bathroom.

Apartment-style
These units can be efficiencies or one- or two-bedroom apartments. Each has a living room, kitchen, and at least one bathroom.

Houses
The University opened its Greek Townhouse Row for eight fraternities and sororities in the fall of 2003, and added individual townhouses around campus for Greek organizations in the fall of 2004. There is also an on-campus "Scholars Village." Students in the Scholars Village design a Living and Learning Community for their house and must participate in activities throughout the year that relate to their community.

Bed Type
Twin beds. Some are bunked, but residence hall staffers can un-bunk the beds. Lofts are not allowed.

Cleaning Service?
Housekeepers clean rooms in freshman dorms once a week, but after that students are on their own. Vacuums are available at some dorms' front desks.

Also Available
GW has several Living and Learning Communities, which provide students with the option to live on the same floor as students with similar interests. Communities focus on topics including film, healthy living, and politics. When students fill out housing preference forms, they can either check the "smoker" or "non-smoker" box. While smoking is allowed in dorm rooms, there are designated smoking and non-smoking rooms according to preference.

Did You Know?

Think only students live in residence halls? You'll find **a few permanent residents** (non-students) living in The West End and The Schenley. The residents lived in the buildings before GW purchased the facilities and converted them into dorms, and they refused to leave their apartments.

A local resident filed a lawsuit against GW for $10 million in May 2003 claiming that **the Ivory Tower dorm was being built partially on his property**, because the building would arch over the property by it's finish. However, the District ruled in April 2004 against the resident.

The Hall on Virginia Avenue, formerly a Howard Johnson hotel, **played a part in the Watergate burglary** that led to the resignation of President Richard Nixon in 1974.

Want to go to GW but don't like living in the city? Live on the Mount Vernon campus, located outside Foggy Bottom. The campus is only a shuttle ride away from Foggy Bottom, and while some students find it anti-social, others love the small classes and intimate living style available there. Non-Mount Vernon residents can also take classes on the campus.

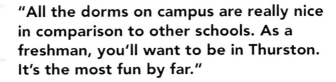

{ **"All the dorms on campus are really nice in comparison to other schools. As a freshman, you'll want to be in Thurston. It's the most fun by far."**

Q "GW is known for its dorms. Most of the residence halls feature a **refrigerator, microwave, Ethernet connections, cable television, and private bathrooms**. The most popular freshman residence hall is Thurston Hall, where more than 1,000 freshmen live. It is not the best-looking building, but is a very social experience. There can be anywhere from two people to a room to six people in a suite. My freshman year, I lived in the Hall on Virginia Avenue (HOVA), which is a renovated Howard Johnson hotel. The rooms were absolutely beautiful—you're living in total luxury. Also, there are more than 400 students in that building, so it's still pretty social. That building is all doubles and triples. At GW, you also have the opportunity to participate in a Living and Learning Community, which has a theme around which your Community Facilitator (similar to a Resident Adviser) will focus activities. For example, we have the 'Press Room,' which focuses on media and journalism. Students in this community go to museums for trips and listen to someone from the White House press corps speak."

Q "Most of the dorms are nice. It depends on what you're looking for in a dorm, because some of the freshman dorms tend to have different personalities. The upperclassman dorms are incredibly nice, like the Dakota and City Hall. They're also building some new ones. **I think that GW has the best housing in the United States**. Second to academics, housing is the best thing."

Q "Dorms are awesome. Stay in the ones that have your own bathroom in the room. Freshman year, almost everyone lives in Thurston, the party dorm. **HOVA is really nice because it's an old Howard Johnson**. Sophomore year, you can live in the Dakota, but it's impossible to get into. But if you can, they're awesome apartments. After that there's New Hall and E Street, but pretty much all other dorms are nasty, small, and dirty."

Q "**The dorms are so nice**. Everyone has a bathroom in his or her own room with a toilet, sink, and shower. Everyone also has his or her own phone and Internet lines, which means that you can talk to your parents and still instant message people at the same time. Thurston is the big freshman dorm. It is a great experience."

Q "With a few exceptions, the dorms here are like palaces. **If you're a freshman, head for HOVA; don't think twice**. The best sophomore and other upperclassman dorms are the Dakota, New Hall, and City Hall. Stay away from the West End, Crawford Hall, and Mitchell Hall."

Q "I lived in Mitchell Hall by a fluke freshman year. It's the only all-single hall on campus, but it's not at all antisocial. It's actually great for freshmen because halls really bond together. My best friend/roommate sophomore year was a girl who lived on my floor in Mitchell. **Everything after freshman year is pretty much apartment-style**, which rocks. I lived in a JBKO double and it was like a little apartment, not a dorm. It's great to have your own kitchen and bathroom, and great closet space."

Q "Everyone should live in Thurston Hall freshman year—it's a dorm for 1,000 college freshmen! Best experience—I am so happy I lived there. The only downfall is that because there are so many students, there are mostly rooms of four and six. City Hall and New Hall are the best upperclassman dorms. City Hall was once a hotel and has a kitchen and living room with a marble-tiled bathroom. **Don't live in Crawford Hall or the Schenley**. They are old, small dorms."

Q "Freshman housing changes, but my first pick would be HOVA. **Thurston can be overwhelming**, and Mitchell is all singles, and I don't know how easy it is to meet people there."

Q "The dorms are okay. **I'd say they all about average out because each one has its ups and downs**. Some are a lot nicer but have poor location. Some are a little rundown but have great location and facilities. It all depends on what is more important to you, but there are options for everyone."

The College Prowler Take On...
Campus Housing

GW's dorms are definitely some of the sweetest in the country—the majority of them are converted apartment buildings or hotels, or recently-built facilities. About half of the freshman class will live in Thurston Hall, GW's largest dorm. Because of its reputation as a "sexually active party dorm," most students who live in Thurston either love it or hate it, with the majority loving every minute. Rooms range from doubles to sixes, and each has a bathroom and one or more walk-in closets. Although they might sound spacious, the rooms are cramped and residents sometimes feel like they're on top of each other. Because more than 1,000 first-years are living together, there's always a party in Thurston, so it can be hard to concentrate on homework there. Among freshmen not ready for the 24-hour fun Thurston has to offer, the Hall on Virginia Avenue is a popular choice. A former Howard Johnson hotel, accommodations are much more spacious than in Thurston. It is also a very social dorm, where students meet, mingle, and party from time to time.

Unlike dorms at some other city schools, GW's are all located very close to or on campus, with only a few exceptions. City Hall and HOVA are one- or two-minute walks outside campus boundaries, and the Aston is a little farther. Many students feel no need to move out of University housing because most of GW's accommodations are so beautiful. The University prides itself on its facilities and residence halls, and purchases and builds dorms regularly.

The College Prowler® Grade on

A high Campus Housing grade indicates that dorms are clean, well-maintained, and spacious. Other determining factors include variety of dorms, proximity to classes, and social atmosphere.

Off-Campus Housing

The Lowdown On...
Off-Campus Housing

Undergrads in Off-Campus Housing:
37%

Best Time to Look for a Place:
Beginning of second semester

Most Popular Area:
Foggy Bottom

Average Rent For:
Studio Apt.: $1,100/month
1BR Apt.: $1,700/month
2BR Apt.: $2,300/month

Students Speak Out On...
Off-Campus Housing

"Living off campus is convenient but very expensive. Since you are in the middle of DC, there are tons of apartments, and a lot of them are very close to campus."

Q "Off-campus housing is very convenient, though not necessarily less expensive than on-campus housing. Being in a major city, there are tons of apartment buildings and even townhouses to rent. That's a decision to make after sophomore year, though, because students have to live on campus until then."

Q "Off-campus housing is really hard to find, really expensive, and almost not worth the trouble. To be honest, residence halls are your best bet because everything is furnished for you, and living there is probably cheaper in the long-run."

Q "It's really convenient to find off-campus housing. Apartment buildings are everywhere, and you can even find some friends and rent out a townhouse. The popular student apartment buildings are the Statesman, Columbia Plaza, the Elise, Claridge House, Letterman House, and the Savoy."

Q "You can find affordable housing off campus, but you give up the Internet connection and free cable. You can find some cheap places off campus, but your best bet is being at least a Metro stop away."

Q "If you have the cash, an apartment isn't hard, but living in the city is expensive."

Q "Off-campus housing is doable, but I don't recommend it. Most of the students stay on campus because it's really nice. **GW has the best housing in the nation, and it's not afraid to admit it**. The first year is basically the only one without apartment-style living—most of the dorms are converted hotels and apartment buildings."

Q "Housing, as in any city, is not convenient. It is usually a headache to find an apartment, but most do after some effort. **It is easier to find off-campus housing in the early summer**, when other students vacate."

Q "Off-campus housing is plentiful but pricey near campus. **Living a Metro ride away will save a lot of money**."

The College Prowler Take On...
Off-Campus Housing

Many off-campus apartments are really close to campus. Popular buildings such as Columbia Plaza, the Empire, Letterman House, and the Statesman are actually located within campus boundaries, while apartment buildings such as Carriage House, Claridge House, and the Savoy are only a few blocks away. Rent can range from $600 to $1,400 per person per month, matching GW's high housing prices, though living off campus is usually harder to find than on-campus housing, which is guaranteed for the first two years. Students are required to live on campus for their freshman and sophomore years, but many get around the rule by saying they have asthma, keep kosher, or cannot afford on-campus living. Those living on-campus do not have to worry about buying any furniture, paying for cable, or getting hooked up to the Internet. However, students living off-campus enjoy their freedom and privacy.

Students at GW find off-campus housing to be a real toss-up. GW's housing accommodations are generally beautiful, so some students prefer to live on-campus all four years, but others want more freedom and do not mind spending the extra few hundred or thousand dollars to furnish a place. Furnished apartments are the best, but they are rare. There are exceptions, though—Claridge House has pretty reasonable prices and offers some partially-furnished rooms. Most on-campus accommodations cost about the same as off-campus housing (before factoring in extra expenses), and apartments are pretty easy to find if students are willing to look hard.

The College Prowler® Grade on

A high grade in Off-Campus Housing indicates that apartments are of high quality, close to campus, affordable, and easy to secure.

Diversity

The Lowdown On...
Diversity

African American:
6%

White:
75%

Asian American:
9%

International:
4%

Hispanic:
5%

Out-of-State:
97%

Native American:
1%

Political Activity

Living in the nation's capital inspires many GW students' interest in the political process. Several have internships on Capitol Hill or at political organizations. The College Democrats and College Republicans also sponsor speakers and events throughout the year. President George W. Bush, Vice President Al Gore, Secretary of State Colin Powell, Presidential Nominee John Kerry, and several senators have spoken at GW within the past few years. Some students are also involved in protests that occur near campus or other activist activities and organizations. The political scene is very present at GW.

Gay Pride

The student body is very open and friendly toward the gay community. Student organizations such as the Out Crowd and GW Pride hold activities and meetings for gay, lesbian, and transgender students. Since there is an active and present gay population at GW, students are willing to accept and understand the gay community's rights and interests.

Economic Status

GW students seem to come from middle to upper-class families. Although many students receive financial aid and are on work study programs, several students complain about all the "rich kids" who like to show off their money. GW is an expensive university that many students' parents can afford outright.

Most Popular Religions

There is a relatively large Jewish population on GW's campus, and a large presence of Jewish-related activities and Greek organizations. There are also several Christian groups, which are generally not as vocal as the Jewish organizations but are still present. The Muslim community hosts several activities throughout the year, including forums on diversity and cultural events. Other groups, including the Sikh Student Association, also host events concerning religion and culture. No single religion dominates campus, but there are plenty of opportunities to become involved with religious organizations or participate in religious events.

Minority Clubs

GW's minority organizations are very active on campus. Asian, Indian, and Middle Eastern religious organizations, among others, hold events and host cultural celebrations throughout the year. Bhangra Blowout, put on by the South Asian Society, is a dance competition held in Washington each year that attracts thousands of college students from across the country. Cultural festivals and shows such as Diwali, Holi, and Alpha Phi Alpha's Step Show attract students, as well. There are also black, Asian, Latino, and Jewish fraternities and sororities, and the University is always welcoming new multicultural fraternities and sororities to campus. Other minority organizations such as several Asian, black, Jewish, Christian and other minority clubs also hold activities on campus.

Students Speak Out On...
Diversity

"We have a large Jewish population and a good amount of international students. There are people from many different states, although the majority are from New Jersey, New York, and Massachusetts."

Q "We have every ethnicity. **We are known for our international students**."

Q "**GW is diverse, supposedly, but it's really not**. It's true that we have students from all over the world, but the groups hang out with each other only. Japanese students only hang out together. Middle Eastern students only hang out together. Indian students only hang out together. Diverse? Yes. Mixed and all hanging out together? No."

Q "GW prides itself on being very diverse, and it is. I found this to be one of the better things about GW because it provides a great atmosphere for learning more about yourself as well as other people's cultures. **There are lots of organizations on campus that cater to diversity** and make it very public for everyone to take part in."

Q "**The campus is pretty diverse for its size**. There are a good number of Jewish, Asian, and Arab students."

Q "The campus is very diverse. **We have so many countries represented at the University**; however, less than 10 percent is African American."

Q "The campus is fairly diverse, and while it may seem a bit divided, I've found that **my friends come from many different backgrounds**."

Q "GW is fairly diverse. **All types of people come to GW**. There are a lot of international students. It's true, though—lots of New Jersey and Long Island kids. But students definitely come from all over."

Q "While the campus is very ethnically diverse, for the most part I've found that **there isn't much interaction between ethnic groups** in a social sense."

The College Prowler Take On...
Diversity

The majority of GW's student body is made up of white students from the East Coast; however, the University has a decent representation of students of different ethnicities, places of origin, and races. Washington, in general, attracts a diverse population. But while GW is a somewhat diverse campus, individual ethnic groups tend to stick together. Asian, black, Jewish, Arab, and Muslim students host cultural events to which the entire GW community is invited. However, the majority of attendees are usually students who are a part of the culture hosting the event, and students usually socialize with those of similar background.

Outside of cultural activities, students have the chance to meet people of other religions and races during class and at social events. International affairs courses attract an ethnically diverse group of interested students, as do certain other types of classes. Most fraternities and sororities are primarily white, but there are students of other backgrounds in the organizations. In addition, there are fraternities and sororities specifically for Asian, black, Latino, and Jewish students.

The College Prowler® Grade on

A high grade in Diversity indicates that ethnic minorities and international students have a notable presence on campus and that students of different economic backgrounds, religious beliefs, and sexual preferences are well-represented.

Guys & Girls

The Lowdown On...
Guys & Girls

Men Undergrads:
44%

Women Undergrads:
56%

Birth Control Available?

Not really . . . GW's Student Health Services does not offer gynecological exams, so it cannot give out long-term prescriptions for birth control. However, the University will give first-time birth control users a one-month prescription until they can make an appointment with a gynecologist. Students are usually referred to the GW Hospital's OB/GYN, located in the same building as Student Health, or Planned Parenthood in the District for birth control. The "morning-after pill," however, is available for $25 at Student Health. Students can also pay $40 for HIV testing at GW—a ridiculous price.

Most Prevalent STDs on Campus

Chlamydia

Gonorrhea

Herpes

Syphilis

Social Scene

GW students definitely like to party, whether on or off campus. Freshman year, the majority of students are very outgoing and excited to meet other students. After freshman year, when students settle in a little more and have a more set group of friends, they are less likely to reach out and meet others. But with so many activities, bars, concerts, and parties on and around campus, it is easy to meet new people and make friends. Yes, there are some stuck-up and snobby people at GW, but there are also many terrific potential friends. Students just have to meet a lot of people to establish a solid group of friends.

Hookups or Relationships?

Most people are not looking for a serious relationship at GW. Freshman year is all about random hookups at parties, clubs, and bars. As students move into sophomore and junior year, some students (especially girls) start looking for something more serious. But it's pretty tough to find a significant other because the majority of students are just looking for fun and casual hookups. In general, GW students are very active and independent people and often say they do not have time for a boyfriend or girlfriend. But there are exceptions to the casual relationship "rule," so keep your eyes peeled.

Did You Know?

Top Places to Find Hotties:

1. Capitol Hill
2. Lerner Health and Wellness Center
3. Georgetown University

Top Places to Hook Up:

1. The monuments at night
2. Thurston Hall, known as one of the most sexually active dorms in the country
3. Kogan Plaza at night
4. Gelman Library stacks
5. Frat parties

Best Place to Meet Guys/Girls

If students are looking for one-night stands, they should check out fraternities, clubs, and bars. Students looking for something a little more serious should think about what kind of girl or guy they want. Campus activities, lectures, and class are great places to find students with similar interests. Smaller apartment and house parties are also good ways to meet people because they are quieter than fraternity parties. Look for non-GW students at work if you intern at an outside organization. Many recent graduates call DC home, and can be potential partners. Also, don't forget about friends of friends.

Dress Code

Because GW is located in a city and many students are from metropolitan areas, most people dress fashionably. Some girls go to class in black pants carrying Prada bags, and many guys head to class in button-down shirts and khakis; but then there is always a stoner passing by who just woke up from a nap wearing a tie-dyed T-shirt and shorts. The majority of students don jeans to go to class, unless it's an 8 a.m.—when students usually straggle into such an early class in sweatpants or even pajamas!

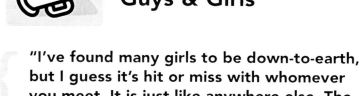
Students Speak Out On...
Guys & Girls

"I've found many girls to be down-to-earth, but I guess it's hit or miss with whomever you meet. It is just like anywhere else. The guys I've met have been really cool."

Q "This is all a personal choice. **I find many girls to be rich and very materialistic**, which some guys have no problem with, but it is one of my pet peeves."

Q "GW, when I applied, was known for pretty girls and okay boys, but I found it different. **You'll find a mix of people.** Some guys are hot, while others are gross."

Q "I would consider GW students better-looking than the average college campus. However, **there are more female students than male**."

Q "**Guys and girls come from all walks of life.** GW is so diverse that you can find just about any type of person that you can imagine."

Q "I love everyone at GW because they are so diverse. However, **many of the hot guys at GW are actually gay**. It's something to keep in mind."

Q "The biggest secret about GW is that **a lot of the students are Jewish**, so sometimes it's a little bit of a religious question when dating. The guys, overall, are pretty nice and definitely hot. The girls are pretty nice. I will admit that there are some really stuck-up girls, but there are some good people at GW."

Q "It all depends on who you come into contact with. **There are attractive people all over the place**. You just need to find them."

Q "If you're a guy coming to GW, points for you because **the ratio of girls to guys is pretty bad on the girl end**. Girls vastly outnumber boys."

Q "I have no comment on the guys, but most of the girls are hot. **I met my girlfriend here and we're still together**, so I'm definitely pleased."

Q "Lots of people on the campus are very snotty and pretentious. It's hard to get over people like that, but you will find them everywhere. Unfortunately, **most of the guys are not hot and completely full of themselves**. But DC is a great place for meeting people, so you never know!"

Q "There are some hot girls, and then there are some not-so-hot girls. As for the guys, since I am a representative of GW, and I will base my opinion on myself; **the guys are extremely hot**."

The College Prowler Take On...
Guys & Girls

The best word to use when describing guys and girls at GW is "average." You'll find very good-looking guys and girls and less attractive individuals, but most students fall in the middle of the spectrum. You have to pick your way through the self-absorbed guys and stuck-up girls, but many GW students are worthy of your friendship. There are a lot of stuck-up people on campus; however, it depends on your attitude. If you take the time to get to know people, most are nice. And those who are more into their Gucci sunglasses and Juicy sweatsuits than your friendship are probably not worth your time.

More than looks, people's passion for the activities in which they are involved make them desirable. There are dateable people in every organization, residence hall, and party, but there are also people who are less attractive. For the most part, the hotties stick together when it comes to fraternities and sororities. The good-looking "bad boys" are in Sigma Alpha Epsilon, and the cute regular Joes are in Kappa Sigma. Kappa Kappa Gamma has the best-looking girls, but they're known for being airheads; other sororities are a real mixture of the good-looking and not-so-good-looking. Hottie or nottie, GW students are very involved in on- and off-campus activities and internships. The cute guy in Sig Ep is not just "that frat guy you see at parties." He is probably also involved in a cultural group, political organization, or sports team. One complaint from the female population however, is that there are fewer guys than girls and that a lot of the guys are gay.

The College Prowler® Grade on

A high grade for Guys indicates that the male population on campus is attractive, smart, friendly, and engaging, and that the school has a decent ratio of guys to girls.

The College Prowler® Grade on

A high grade for Girls not only implies that the women on campus are attractive, smart, friendly, and engaging, but also that there is a fair ratio of girls to guys.

Athletics

The Lowdown On...
Athletics

Athletic Division:
NCAA Division I

Conference:
Atlantic 10

School Mascot:
Colonial

**Males Playing
Varsity Sports:**
172 (4%)

**Females Playing
Varsity Sports:**
243 (5%)

→

Men's Varsity Sports:

Baseball

Basketball

Cheerleading

Cross-Country

Golf

Rowing

Soccer

Squash

Swimming/Diving

Tennis

Water Polo

Women's Varsity Sports:

Basketball

Cheerleading

Cross-Country

Gymnastics

Lacrosse

Rowing

Soccer

Softball

Squash

Swimming/Diving

Tennis

Volleyball

Water Polo

Club Sports:

Badminton

Baseball

Capoeira Angola

Cycling

Fencing

Field Hockey (women)

Ice Hockey (men)

Ice Hockey (women)

JKA Karate

Kendo

Lacrosse (men)

Lacrosse (women)

Martial Arts Club

Paintball

Racquetball

Roller Hockey

Rugby (men)

Rugby (women)

Sailing

Shotokan Karate of America

Soccer (men)

Soccer (women)

Tae Kwon Do

Ultimate Frisbee (men)

Ultimate Frisbee (women)

Volleyball

Intramurals:

3-on-3 Basketball
6-on-6 Volleyball
5-on-5 Basketball
7-on-7 Soccer
A-10 Shootout
Arena Football
Dodgeball
Doubles Bowling
Doubles Foosball
Doubles Tennis
Floor Hockey
Mount Vernon Indoor Soccer
Racquetball Singles
Singles Tennis
Softball
Sports Trivia
Squash
Table Tennis
Team Bowling
Team Wiffleball
Volleyball Pre-Season

Athletic Fields

Soccer/lacrosse field at the Mount Vernon campus

Baseball field at Barcroft Field in Arlington, VA

Most Popular Sports

Men's basketball

Men's soccer

Rowing

Overlooked Teams

Golf

Gymnastics

Water polo

Women's basketball

Best Place to Take a Walk

Potomac River

Around the Monuments

Getting Tickets

Students receive free tickets to all sporting events.

Gyms/Facilities

Lerner Health and Wellness Center

One of GW's newest and most aesthetically pleasing facilities, the Health and Wellness Center is where non-varsity athletes on Foggy Bottom work out. There is a spacious cardio room with bikes, elliptical machines, rowing machines, step machines, and treadmills. The weight room in the back is rather small, but it provides students with different free weight and weight machine options. Some students also enjoy the group fitness classes, which cost about $60 per semester and include cycling, kickboxing, and step classes. The Hell Well also has a pool, racquetball courts, an Einstein Bros. Bagels, personal trainers for a fee, and massages for a fee, among other amenities. It is the best place to work out on campus.

The Smith Center

The Smith Center is a facility used primarily by varsity athletes. Older than Hell Well, the Smith Center offers fewer machines because it does not accommodate as many students. There is also a pool, and some one-credit fitness classes are held there.

Mount Vernon Athletic Complex

Since Mount Vernon is located outside the city, it has plenty of space for outdoor athletic fields. The lacrosse, softball, soccer, and tennis teams call Mount Vernon home. The beautiful fields are perfect for team practices, and they provide GW students with the opportunity to watch outdoor sports nearby. In the summertime, students can use the outdoor Mount Vernon pool for free. GW also has some exercise equipment available on the Mount Vernon campus, so residents do not necessarily have to travel to Foggy Bottom to get in shape.

Students Speak Out On...
Athletics

> **"Some people get into the varsity sports and others don't. It's the same with intramurals. It is all about what you get involved in."**

Q "Sports, just like everything else at GW, have their own loyal group of supporters, but they do not dominate the scene. The basketball team is probably our biggest sport, but **GW is a school that definitely encourages individualism**. Everyone does his own thing, and the experience you have here is what you make of it. They have intramural sports, which are a lot of fun to play."

Q "GW is Division I athletics, but we do not have a football team. **For the most part, people attend basketball games**, but usually not other sports. Intramural sports are relatively popular. GW also offers one-credit exercise and sports activities classes in everything from squash to horseback riding, golf to weight training."

Q "Sports are not a main part of GW at all, although they are Division I. People play sports, but no one is really into it. I know some of my friends participated in intramurals for fun. **GW doesn't have a football team**, but people are pretty big on basketball."

Q "**Varsity and intramural sports aren't huge**, but many do take part in them. We are a basketball school, and the games are a big thing. Everyone goes!"

Q "**GW's best varsity sport is women's gymnastics**, but nobody here really cares about that. The biggest varsity sport at GW is basketball and the games can be fun, but most of the student body here is pretty much apathetic toward sports. Being an urban school with a lack of greenery and a football team might have something to do with it."

Q "I'm not the most athletic person, but even I realize that GW is really lacking on spirit. **I think we need a really great sports team or teams to rally behind** and unite the school with some GW spirit and pride. That sounds really corny, but I think it's important."

Q "Sports are not a big thing by any means at GW. Our basketball team isn't that good, but I enjoy going to games. Lots of people don't show up, though. Besides basketball, **we have a good crew team that competes with other schools** in the area, and people enjoying watching the team."

Q "GW is not a big sports school. The gym is usually more packed than the basketball games. Intramural sports are not so popular either. **We do have several professional sports teams to watch, as well**. Going to see the Wizards or Capitals is always fun."

The College Prowler Take On...
Athletics

GW is not a sports enthusiast's dream come true. There is not much school spirit at GW, perhaps because the University has no football team; its main sport is men's basketball. The games can get packed during the season, and definitely during the finals, but a lot of students are apathetic about other teams, including the very talented women's basketball team. Most non-varsity athletes do not attend games other than men's basketball, if that. Intramural sports are popular and pretty casual. Club teams are more competitive—the GW teams travel to other universities to play. People involved in sports at these levels say they have a lot of fun in the mildly competitive atmosphere.

GW tries to promote spirit among its students, but the efforts often fail. The University used to hold a traditional "Midnight Madness" activity each fall, which was like a huge pep rally—dancers, jugglers, and musicians performed before the basketball teams came out for their first practice of the season at midnight. But the University decided to cut the program for fall 2003 because students were leaving early and got bored with all the hubbub. The women's basketball team, which has done well recently, is basically ignored—almost no one attends games. Sports fans can attend outside games at the University of Maryland or watch one of several professional teams in the area. At GW, there are opportunities to play and watch sports, but if early morning tailgate parties before jam-packed football games is what you crave, then you'll be better off looking elsewhere.

The College Prowler® Grade on

A high grade in Athletics indicates that students have school spirit, that sports programs are respected, that games are well-attended, and that intramurals are a prominent part of student life.

Nightlife

The Lowdown On...
Nightlife

Club and Bar Prowler:
Popular Nightlife Spots!

Club Crawler:

There are some really great clubs in Washington that are filled with college students. Most students go to clubs their freshman year, and then switch over to the bar scene once they turn 21 or acquire fake IDs. The majority of clubs are 18 to enter, but some are 21-and-up. GW students flock to clubs more when a fraternity or

(Club Crawler, continued)

group sponsors a party. There are usually flyers passed out around campus, in dorms, and near the Marvin Center letting students know which clubs are "hot spots" for a particular night.

Andalu

1214 18th St. NW,
Dupont Circle

(202) 785-2922

Andalu plays a lot of house, trance, and international music, creating a different vibe from most clubs and bars around.

➜

(Andalu, continued)

Catering to a mostly European crowd, Andalu attracts GW students because of its dark atmosphere and interesting clientele. Drinks are expensive, people dress well, and you are likely to hear several languages being spoken. Andalu is a nice change from GW's scene.

Bravo Bravo

1001 Connecticut Ave. NW,
Dupont Circle

(202) 223-5330

Bravo Bravo is a huge, primarily Latin club popular enough to have been around for years (not too common when it comes to DC clubs). On weekends, when Bravo is open until 4 a.m., expect to find it packed pretty much all night. As with most major DC clubs, don't show up looking like you just rolled out of bed.

Five

1214B 18th St. NW,
Dupont Circle

(202) 331-7123

A mixture of a traditional club and a lounge, Five plays music ranging from hip hop to reggae, from funk to dance or mellow house beats. The dance floor is usually pretty crowded, but many club goers hang out in the lounge areas instead of racing toward the floor. Five is a favorite among GW students, and the club often charges no cover.

Lulu's Club Mardi Gras

1217 22nd St. NW,
Foggy Bottom

(202) 861-5858

Always a blast, Lulu's often hosts several theme nights and parties. Past events include appearances by cast members from MTV's *Real World Las Vegas* and a contest to find the next *Girls Gone Wild*. The large club has a dance floor and a few bars downstairs and a VIP section upstairs. It is usually crowded on Thursdays.

MCCXXIII

1223 Connecticut Ave. NW,
Dupont Circle

(202) 822-1800

Pronounced 1223 by those who can't read Roman numerals, MCCXXIII is a sleek, upscale club popular among GW students. Attractive men and women dance along to decent music on the top of a large bar. Upstairs, people can chill at a bar and catwalk that overlooks the entire club.

Platinum

915 F St. NW,
Penn Quarter

(202) 393-3555

Platinum is housed in a huge, elegant building, formerly a bank; it even features a bar in place of teller windows. The club plays mostly house and trance, and drinks and cover are typically very expensive. Come well-dressed, with a full wallet.

→

Tequila Beach

1115 F St. NW,
Downtown
(202) 393-5463

Tequila Beach is mostly known for Fiesta Fridays, the bar's weekly beach-themed college house party. Domestics and shooters are $3 at the event, which is 18-and-up (though 21 to drink, obviously). The club plays mostly hip hop and dance music, and caters to a primarily college-age crowd.

Bar Prowler:

Once students turn 21, they love the bar scene near GW. Located a few minutes from campus, bars on the edge of Dupont Circle on M Street are student favorites. Adams Morgan is also great because it boasts a strip of fun bars. Georgetown is a good area to explore, and you can usually find students from Georgetown and American Universities there. If you are motivated enough to want a beer but too lazy to go very far, several bars are only a few steps from campus, including Lindy's Red Lion and Froggy Bottom Pub. Located right near campus, they're relatively casual and always chill.

Brickskeller

1623 22nd St. NW,
Dupont Circle
(202) 293-1885

Though it seems at first like a pleasant but small hole-in-the-wall, Brickskeller can boast something not many bars can—it's in the Guinness Book of World Records, due to the enormity of its beer selection (at the time it was awarded its title, Brickskeller carried 1,072 commercial beers). What's more, quite of few of these are reasonably priced around $3, making the bar a decent place to visit whether you're looking for a cheap domestic or a $20 imported Trappist.

Café Citron

1343 Connecticut Ave., NW,
Dupont Circle
(202) 530-8844

Citron is a half-bar, half-lounge that offers much more reasonable prices (on food, and often on drinks) than its Dupont peers. The bar features live music and DJs, and a flamenco show on Mondays. After 10 p.m., Citron is 21-and-up.

→

The Common Share

2003 18th St. NW,
Adams Morgan

(202) 588-7180

The main draw at the Common Share is the fact that most of its drinks are priced regularly at $2, which is almost impossible to beat in DC The only problem is that the downstairs—where the bar is—is tiny and usually incredibly crowded. The upstairs is much more spacious, and offers a pool table and art on the walls, but again, doesn't contain a bar. Overall, it's a decent place to start a night out, assuming you don't mind fighting your way to the bar every time you buy a round.

The ESPN Zone

555 12th St. NW,

Downtown

(202) 783-3776

Featuring games and dozens of TVs turned to sporting events (including one 16-foot screen), ESPN Zone is a great place for 18-and-over students to catch a game. Be aware, though, that during certain times of day (NFL Sundays, for instance), the establishment imposes a $10 per person, per hour minimum.

Felix

2406 18th St. NW,
Adams Morgan

(202) 483-3549

Students will feel cool and sophisticated as they sit on velvet couches sipping martinis in one of Adams Morgan's sleeker bars. At Felix, GW students can mingle with the older clients who also frequent the bar. If students want to drink in high style and meet some older men and women, they should head over to Felix, but bar hoppers must remember to check out some of Adams Morgan's other great, casual bars while in the area.

Froggy Bottom Pub

2142 Pennsylvania Ave. NW,
Foggy Bottom

(202) 338-3000

When bar hoppers approach Froggy, they have two choices: follow the "Grub" sign upstairs to the eating area or the "Pub" sign downstairs to the bar area. Choose the latter if you're looking for the typical college bar. Adjacent to GW's campus, students come to Froggy after class or at night for some close-to-home partying. Students drink beer out of plastic cups, play pool, and chill with friends. Froggy is very casual, so students can walk in wearing sweatpants and feel comfortable.

Front Page

1313 New Hampshire Ave. NW, Dupont Circle

(202) 296-6500

A must on Thursday nights, Front Page has the best drink specials around—Coronas and Miller Lights are $1.50 from 5 p.m. until closing. The bar is a hotspot with the after-work and after-class crowd, so happy hours prove to be a blast. Front Page is a GW favorite because of its close proximity to campus, good music, hot and sweaty environment, and decent population of college students from around the city. Georgetown and American students frequent Front Page, as well.

Hawk 'n' Dove

329 Pennsylvania Ave. SE, Capitol Hill

(202) 543-3300

Touting itself as "DC's oldest Irish bar," Hawk 'n' Dove is a more sedate, laid-back alternative to bars in Dupont or Foggy Bottom; the patrons are mostly political staffers and other Capitol Hill employees. The $9 breakfast, available at night, is a sizable meal for the price. Drink specials range from $1.50 Coors Light bottles on Mondays to $3.25 microbrews on Fridays.

Lucky Bar

1221 Connecticut Ave., Dupont Circle

(202) 331-3733

Like many other Dupont Circle bars, Lucky Bar offers decent drink specials—$2 Budweiser on Fridays, $1 Rolling Rock during happy hour. It does offer something those other bars don't, however: soccer. Serving a diverse, international crowd, Lucky Bar shows soccer matches on its TVs almost exclusively, particularly for important World Cup or Champions League matches (during which there's usually a drink minimum).

Madhatter

1831 M St. NW, Dupont Circle

(202) 833-1495

Madhatter is a GW favorite and one of the best bars in the area. Every night of the week, but especially on Thursdays and Fridays, GW students are at the Hatter dancing to their favorite tunes and drinking the night away. The music is fantastic at Madhatter, where everyone's favorite DJ alternates classic rock hits and pop tunes. If you're looking for a bar with a causal environment and a lot of dancing GW students, Madhatter is the place to go. On Fridays, Budweiser and Bud Lights are only $2 all night, and rail drinks are $2.50.

McFadden's

2401 Pennsylvania Ave. NW,
Georgetown

(202) 223-2338

McFadden's opened in spring 2003 and instantly became one of the hottest bars in the area. On weekend nights, the line to get in usually winds around the block. McFadden's is casual but somewhat upscale, offering good drinks, good friends, and good times. Tuesday's dollar beer night is especially popular. But don't try using a fake ID—Metro Police are constantly patrolling McFadden's because of its popularity.

Rhino Bar & Pumphouse

3295 M St. NW,
Georgetown

(202) 333-3150

A great sports bar (affiliated with the Red Sox, among others) with great bartenders, Rhino was included among the 20 best dive bars in the country by *Stuff* magazine. The bar offers 25 cent wings during football games on Saturday and Sunday (the price drops to 10 cents during Monday Night Football). Bud and Bud Light are $2 on Tuesdays, which is also poker night (with no buy-in).

Sign of the Whale

1825 M St. NW,
Dupont Circle

(202) 785-1110

Located two doors down from Madhatter, Sign of the Whale is usually a blast. GW students sometimes refer to this classic-looking bar as a "dive," but that does not stop them from downing cheap drinks and hanging out with friends. The bar sometimes attracts an older crowd, but there are usually plenty of GW students on hand. Plus, Sign has good food. On certain nights, there are half-price burgers and chicken sandwich specials, which go well with a beer.

Tequila Grill

1990 K St. NW,
Downtown

(202) 588-1300

A popular Mexican restaurant with pretty good food, Tequila Grill's main draw is its happy hour. Every weekday from 3:30 to 7:30, drinks are half-price and margaritas are $2.50; there are various other drink specials throughout the week, as well, (including $1.50 Coronas on Thursdays). Expect a decent after-work crowd all week during happy hour.

The Third Edition

2335 18th St. NW,
Georgetown

(202) 333-3700

The Third Edition, primarily
a Georgetown hangout, is a
trendy, popular spot—equal
parts bar, club, and restaurant.
The trendiness and popularity
have their price, though; the
Third Edition certainly isn't DC's
cheapest nightspot. Draft beer
is in the $5 range, and dinner
runs about $35 per person.
Still, the place has plenty to
offer if you're inclined to spend
some cash.

Tom Tom

2335 18th St. NW,
Adams Morgan

(202) 588-1300

Tom Tom is right in the heart
of Adams Morgan, a beloved
spot for students looking
to bar hop. Tom Tom is a
relatively casual bar that is
usually packed with students
and 20-somethings looking
for music, drinks, and dancing.
After hitting up Tom Tom and
other Adams Morgan bars such
as the Reef, head over to Pizza
Mart for a late-night snack. The
restaurant offers huge slices of
pizza that students gobble up
on their way home from a night
of partying.

Student Favorites:

Froggy Bottom Pub
Front Page
Madhatter
McFadden's
Sign of the Whale

Useful Resources for Nightlife:

City Paper
Floors of Thurston Hall
Time Out Guide to Washington DC
The *Washington Post*
The *Washingtonian*

Bars Close At:

2 a.m. in general
3 a.m. in Adams Morgan

Primary Areas with Nightlife:

Adams Morgan
Area adjacent to campus
Dupont Circle
Georgetown

Cheapest Place to Get a Drink:

The Common Share
Front Page

Other Places to Check Out:

Adams Mill
Babylon
Brass Monkey
Café Citron
Cities
Daedalus
Helix
Lindy's Red Lion
Lucky Bar
Madam's Organ
The Reef
Rhino Bar
Singapore Bistro
Third Edition

Favorite Drinking Games:

Beer Pong
Card games, especially Kings
Flip Cup
Never Have I Ever
Power Hour
Quarters

What to Do if You're Not 21

The majority of DC's clubs allow students in if they are 18 years old. Fun, traditional clubs such as Bravo Bravo, Platinum, Babylon, and Tequila Beach all admit students who are 18 or older. Singapore Bistro is also a popular place to hang out, and fraternities holding events there often do not check IDs very carefully. Students can also check out the 9:30 Club, a relatively small concert venue that attracts some big names such as Justin Timberlake, Sister Hazel, Marilyn Manson, Ben Kweller, and Dashboard Confessional. The Black Cat is another bar and concert venue that has some theme nights such as "Brit Pop Night" and "Indie Rock Night" that 18-year-olds can attend. The ESPN Zone, a sports bar with televisions that broadcast games and arcade games, is a good place for the 18-and-up crowd to mingle with 21-year-olds. DO NOT use a fake at Lulu's, McFadden's, Tequila Grill, and most places in Georgetown if you don't want to get arrested. Going to jail for the night and getting locked up with criminals is not a pretty picture.

Organization Parties

Fraternities often throw parties in their houses, or at off-campus locations if they do not have houses. Most frats and some other groups also host parties occasionally at clubs, and these events are promoted throughout the week.

Frats

See the Greek section!

Students Speak Out On...
Nightlife

"Nightlife is usually really good. Fraternities and whoever else throw parties all the time. There are bars and clubs everywhere, so there is always something to do. Madhatter is a GW staple, and Front Page."

Q "I think GW and DC have a huge selection of bars that cater to every possible taste. **I never had trouble finding a fun bar or club** while I was there, and most are within a short distance from campus. Usually it is within walking distance, but sometimes it is a short cab or Metro ride—it is no big deal. DC has hundreds of thousands of clubs, bars, and restaurants. The possibilities are endless."

Q "Being in a major city, DC has so many nightlife options. Some of the very casual bars are Madhatter, Froggy Bottom Pub, Lindy's Red Lion, Brickskeller, Bravo Bravo, and Sign of the Whale. All of those are very close to campus. Right at the edge of Georgetown is an area called the Waterfront, which has two popular outdoor bars during the summer. You'll find that **there's always someone promoting something for Thursday nights**, and that turns into the place to be."

Q "The bars and clubs are a lot of fun. The biggest night out for most people is Thursday. Usually, on two nights a weekend, people promote a spot to go out. **There has been a major crackdown in DC regarding underage drinking**; other than that, the bars are awesome. It's not like a state school where there are only a couple places to go. You could go to a different bar every night for four years and still not get to all of them."

Q "In Georgetown, I recommend the Third Edition and Rhino Bar. There are several others. **Adams Morgan has a whole strip of bars and restaurants**, and some of them don't card. Dupont also has some cool bars, and on campus, there is Lindy's Red Lion and Froggy Bottom Pub."

Q "All you are ever going to do on the weekends is go to clubs and bars, although it will mostly be clubs during your freshman year since you won't be 21 yet. **Clubs change depending on what is being promoted**. It's usually about $15 or cheaper to get in. If you have a fake ID, your options definitely open up, but right now, DC police are cracking down on them, so I wouldn't use one in Georgetown because it will definitely be taken away."

Q "The social scene at GW largely revolves around bars and clubs, which is not my scene. I prefer a chill house party or just hanging out with friends. **The house party scene at GW is weak**—make that extremely weak if you live near or are familiar with any of the big state schools."

Q "**You can always find a frat party on campus to go to**, and they are fun, but they are never the focus of attention on a weekend. There are lots of bars and clubs around DC that GW students go to. I like Madhatter, Front Page, Felix, Café Citron, Hawk 'n' Dove, and Andalu. Other popular clubs are MCCXXIII, Lucky Bar, and Five."

The College Prowler Take On...
Nightlife

Because GW is located in the city, off-campus bars are more a part of the social scene than on-campus parties are. Party nights are Tuesdays (for upperclassmen), Thursdays, Fridays, and Saturdays. GW traditionally has offered few Friday classes, so students go out late on Thursday evenings, which, for most 21-year-olds, equals happy hour. Many students frequent a local bar—Lulu's and Front Page are good choices—around 5 or 6 p.m. for specially-priced drinks. After a little "happy houring," students usually go home and rest, then get ready for a night of bar or club hopping around 11 p.m. Freshman year, most students go to fraternity parties or other on-campus get-togethers on weekends. Freshmen also go to clubs because most allow students ages 18 or older.

Nightlife in Washington is fantastic, with many clubs and bars to explore that cater to different people's preferences. But GW students tend to frequent the same bars, meaning students see other students wherever they go. The edge of Dupont Circle is one of the most popular areas for GW students to hang out and bar hop. Madhatter, Front Page, Sign of the Whale, Rumors, and Lucky Bar are all located there. Front Page has great Thursday night specials, Madhatter plays the best music of any bar around, and Sign of the Whale is a typical college bar. For students not interested in the bar or club scene, there are other options. Hit up a friend's apartment party, take in a show, go to a movie or jazz club, hang out at a coffee bar—the possibilities are endless. Washington offers top-notch nightlife, whether you're looking for a loud bar or a quiet, late-night music fest.

The College Prowler® Grade on

A high grade in Nightlife indicates that there are many bars and clubs in the area that are easily accessible and affordable. Other determining factors include the number of options for the under-21 crowd and the prevalence of house parties.

Greek Life

The Lowdown On...
Greek Life

Number of Fraternities: 15	**Undergrad Men in Fraternities:** 15%
Number of Sororities: 8	**Undergrad Women in Sororities:** 13%

→

Fraternities on Campus:

Alpha Epsilon Pi
APES (not recognized by GW)
Beta Theta Pi
Kappa Sigma
Lambda Chi Alpha
Phi Kappa Psi
Phi Sigma Kappa
Pi Kappa Alpha
Pi Kappa Phi
Sigma Alpha (not recognized by GW)
Sigma Alpha Mu (not recognized by GW)
Sigma Nu
Sigma Phi Epsilon
Tau Kappa Epsilon
Theta Delta Chi

Sororities on Campus:

Alpha Delta Pi
Alpha Epsilon Phi
Alpha Phi
Delta Gamma
Kappa Kappa Gamma
Phi Sigma Sigma
Sigma Delta Tau
Sigma Kappa

Other Greek Organizations:

Interfraternity Council
Multicultural Greek Council
National Pan-Hellenic Council
Panhellenic Association

Multicultural Colonies:

Alpha Phi Alpha
Delta Phi Omega
Delta Sigma
Kappa Alpha Psi
Lambda Pi Chi
Lambda Upsilon Lambda
Pi Delta Psi
Sigma Beta Rho
Sigma Lambda Upsilon
Sigma Psi Zeta
Theta Sorority Inc.
Zeta Phi Beta

Did You Know?

 Several fraternities operate off-campus and are known as **"underground" fraternities**. Sigma Alpha Epsilon (SAE), Sigma Alpha Mu (Sammy), and the "APES" fraternities are not recognized by GW. They either got kicked off campus, were turned down when organization leaders asked the University for recognition, or never sought recognition. These fraternities do not have to abide by the University's rules and cannot reside in on-campus fraternity houses.

GW opened a **Greek Townhouse Row** for the fall of 2003. Five sororities and three fraternities inhabit the multimillion-dollar complex. This was the first instance in which sororities had their own houses.

Each year, Lambda Chi Alpha hosts a "**Watermelon Fest**," when members of fraternities and sororities compete in activities. Each organization pays an entrance fee, which is donated to charity.

The fraternity Alpha Epsilon Pi was kicked off campus in early 2001 **because of hazing**. The same group of guys soon became initiated members of the Zeta Beta Tau fraternity because they were no longer AEPis. But the ZBT group soon lost its recognition because of more occurrences of hazing. Now, some of the former AEPis/ZBTs are members of an underground fraternity dubbed "APES." In fall 2002, a new group of guys re-started AEPi and have nothing to do with the original AEPis, ZBTs, or the "APES."

Students Speak Out On...
Greek Life

"Sometimes sorority girls can be a little cliquey, but it's not a big deal. I haven't gone to frat parties that much, but there is always someone you know who can invite you if it is your thing."

Q "Greek life is present at GW, but by no means does it dominate the social scene. Then again, it depends on whom you talk to. If you get involved, it will probably dominate your social scene, but I never got into it and never felt the need to. **There are a lot of people who don't get involved and just do their own thing**."

Q "Greek life is there, and I have a couple friends in frats and sororities, but it isn't the center of activity at GW. However, **the school is trying to bring Greek life closer to campus**. They built a Townhouse Row on campus a few years ago where eight frats and sororities are living."

Q "Greek life does not dominate the social scene; rather, it has its own social scene distinct from the general clubs and bars. Greek life is great; **there are tons of great options for all different types of people**, and houses are generally open and receptive to all sorts of visitors and prospective members. However, it seems to me that sororities are horrible at GW."

Q "I'd say a decent percentage of the undergraduate population is involved in fraternity or sorority life. Greek life is something that you have as an option at GW, but in no way does it dominate the social scene. **Being in a major city, there are too many other things to do**."

Q "There is a Greek life at GW. I am not a part of it or a huge fan, but I would encourage you to rush and see for yourself. **GW really doesn't have a 'go Greek or go home' atmosphere**."

Q "Greek life is great. Greeks do not dominate the campus, but they are a significant force. **I was in a sorority and loved it**, not just for the social aspects but because the Greek community was small then and is continually growing. It's a great part of campus life to experience and be a part of."

Q "I love GW, but when I go to visit my friends at state schools, **I really wish we had serious Greek life instead of GW's sad, fake Greek life**. If you don't want to go Greek, don't worry; it doesn't rule life at all. There's way too much to go out and do to have to depend on Greeks."

The College Prowler Take On...
Greek Life

Greek life does not dominate GW's social scene, but rather adds another flavor to the social dish. Because there are so many organizations to join and jobs and internships to be had in Washington, the majority of students do not feel the need to join a fraternity or sorority. There are also so many nightlife options—bars, clubs, and on- and off-campus parties—that frat parties do not control the social scene. For those involved, Greek life is a lot of fun and very worthwhile. Members attend formals and date parties, meet guys and girls from other frats and sororities, and get a lot of cool clothing with Greek letters on them. It is also a great way to get involved in community service.

If you're not involved—and 86 percent of students are not—you can still go to frat parties and be friends with members of the Greek community. Girls can always get into frat parties, and guys usually do not have a problem, either. Some frats and sororities are very exclusive, but the ones that throw big parties usually are not. Although GW says it wants to promote Greek life on campus, the University is very strict with fraternities and sororities and has several rules concerning parties. As a result, groups continue to get kicked off campus and organization leaders have spoken out against the University's harsh rules.

The College Prowler® Grade on

A high grade in Greek Life indicates that sororities and fraternities are not only present, but also active on campus. Other determining factors include the variety of houses available and the respect the Greek community receives from the rest of the campus.

Drug Scene

The Lowdown On...
Drug Scene

Most Prevalent Drugs on Campus:
Alcohol

Cocaine

Marijuana

Liquor-Related Referrals:
388

Drug-Related Referrals:
99

Drug Counseling Programs:
The Center for Alcohol and other Drug Education offers three programs for students who have had alcohol or drug violations: Time Out, Educated Choices, and Last Call. Students attend one or more workshops or private counseling, depending on the severity of the violation, and write about their experiences.

Students Speak Out On...
Drug Scene

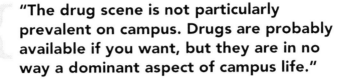

"The drug scene is not particularly prevalent on campus. Drugs are probably available if you want, but they are in no way a dominant aspect of campus life."

Q "Drugs are not really big on campus, although they are definitely present. **I never got involved in the stuff** and never felt pressured to, even though I have numerous friends who use them."

Q "**There are drugs**. They are easy to get, from what I have heard and seen, but the majority of kids are not drug addicts."

Q "It depends on what you want. **If you want to smoke, you will meet smokers**. If you are straight-edged and don't smoke or drink, you will find people who are like that as well. It depends on who you hang out with."

Q "I have heard there is a cocaine problem on campus, but I don't know much about it. **There is a lot of pot and some ecstasy that I know of, but I'm not sure what else**. If you are looking for it, it's there, and if you are trying to avoid it, you can—I have for the past four years."

Q "Well, since it's a pretty rich school, I've heard that cocaine is pretty big. I don't particularly partake in that, so I can't tell you for sure. Obviously, weed is everywhere. This is a pretty big city; **you can find what you want if that's your game**. I think, basically, if you want to get involved with drugs, you can; if you don't, it's easy not to. Simple as that."

Q "Drugs are there if you want them, but they're not the center of social life, per se. A lot of kids smoke weed and some particular groups do use coke. **Ecstasy is not very popular anymore**, and harder stuff is around but not big."

Q **"I think you will find what you are looking for**. If you just want to drink, you will find those friends. If you want to smoke, you can find friends that do, too. Anything more? There are people into that. You can avoid what you want to, as well as find what you are looking for."

The College Prowler Take On...
Drug Scene

There are plenty of students who do drugs at GW—most commonly, students smoke pot, drink alcohol, and smoke cigarettes. If you walk down any floor in Thurston Hall, you'll notice the smell of marijuana drifting out from under a door. A lot of students talk about, sell, and smoke pot on a regular basis. The *GW Hatchet*, the University's student newspaper, even called its 2003 April Fools edition the *BongHit*, which many students and parents found hysterical because they do or did smoke. But for students who are not interested in drugs, there is rarely any pressure to join in; people mostly associate with people who share their views on drugs.

Alcohol is the most popular "drug" on campus. GW students love getting drunk; many are taken to the GW Hospital each week. Students also smoke cigarettes everywhere—in bars and clubs, at parties, walking down the street, and hanging out in front of GW buildings. Study drugs such as Adderall and Ritalin are very popular on campus. Students pop these prescription pills before a long night at the library so they can stay up and write a paper or cram for an exam. There are some harder drugs on campus, such as cocaine and ecstasy, but everyone knows which social circles use those harder drugs, and staying away from them is very easy. Harder drugs are definitely not as visible as alcohol, pot, and study drugs.

The College Prowler® Grade on

A high grade in the Drug Scene indicates that drugs are not a noticeable part of campus life; drug use is not visible, and no pressure to use them seems to exist.

Campus Strictness

The Lowdown On...
Campus Strictness

What Are You Most Likely to Get Caught Doing on Campus?
- Drinking underage
- Bringing food or drinks into the library
- Smoking marijuana in the dorms
- Using a fake ID

Campus Strictness

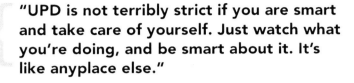

> "UPD is not terribly strict if you are smart and take care of yourself. Just watch what you're doing, and be smart about it. It's like anyplace else."

Q "**Students caught drinking illegally or using drugs on campus face stiff penalties**, including eviction from student housing or expulsion. The University Police Department (UPD) is strict in enforcing all University codes."

Q "Campus police are only strict about drinking and drugs in freshman residence halls. Otherwise, they are very lenient. For example, **if they break up a house party, they do not write down names**."

Q "GW is a pretty strict campus. I got an alcohol violation—that was kind of a slap on the wrist. But **your first time with pot in the dorms, you get kicked out of housing**. So, read over the policy when you get it."

Q "**UPD can be a real pain**. There has recently been a big anti-underage drinking push in DC. Basically, just be careful about it; people usually get caught when they forget to hide bottles before opening doors."

Q "If you are caught in the dorms, officials are very strict. I had a friend who tried marijuana for the first time in Thurston Hall, and he got busted and kicked off campus. But **there are students who smoke every day for six months and never get caught**. For your first drinking violation, you are charged $25 and one alcohol session. It only gets worse after that."

Q "If you are caught, you definitely get into trouble. Freshman halls are supposed to be dry, so they are stricter there. Upperclassman halls are less strict. **Don't be dumb and get caught**."

Q "There is a lot of drinking on campus, and although **the police catch a lot of people**, there is still a lot of drinking going on at the social level."

The College Prowler Take On...
Campus Strictness

GW's policies concerning drugs and alcohol are very strict. If violators are caught drinking (and University Police officers regularly patrol the dorms and respond to noise complaints), they pay a fine and attend alcohol awareness class for the first two violations. The third time, students can be kicked out of housing. Drug-wise, the first time a student is caught, he gets kicked out of housing and receives no refund. Getting caught drinking the first time or two is not the end of the world—it happens to many students. However, students do not want to jeopardize their housing privileges or end up paying for on-campus housing while being forced to live off campus. Students should be careful and leave a party if it is getting too loud. Most upperclassman dorms such as City and New halls are not patrolled as regularly as Thurston or other freshman dorms.

GW seems doubly strict because of the strong Metropolitan Police presence at off-campus parties and bars and clubs. MPD has recently been trying to crack down on underage drinking. If an officer catches an underage person drinking or using a fake ID, he is off to jail for the night. Students should not stop going to parties and bars, but they need to be smart. They should leave if a party is too loud and avoid using fake IDs at bars with a reputation for being strict or having an ID scanner.

B-

The College Prowler® Grade on

A high Campus Strictness grade implies an overall lenient atmosphere; police and RAs are fairly tolerant, and the administration's rules are flexible.

Parking

The Lowdown On...
Parking

Student Parking Lot?
Yes

Freshmen Allowed to Park?
Yes

Parking Permit Cost:
$710 per semester

GW Parking Services:
(202) 994-7275
www.parking.gwu

Did You Know?

Best Places to Find a Parking Spot
• GW parking garages

Good Luck Getting a Parking Spot Here!
• Adams Morgan
• Georgetown

Students Speak Out On...
Parking

"It's hard to park, so do not bring a car. I decided to wait to bring a car just to see how it was for a year, and now I don't want to or need to."

"I lived in DC for a year after school, and I never once wanted a car or ever regretted not having one. Cars are just a hassle in DC. **Parking is expensive, and you'll rarely, if ever, use your car**."

"Parking is very difficult on campus. GW does not recommend that students bring their own car. There is **honestly nowhere to even drive** if you have a car. GW does own and operate parking garages, but it's expensive."

"**Not many people have cars on campus**. Parking is a pain. A car isn't really needed. Yeah, it is nice to have at times, but the Metro and cabs get you where you need to go."

"Not many people bring cars; it's really not necessary. **GW charges a lot to park on the premises**, and otherwise you have to deal with bad street parking."

"**I would not bring a car**. Parking is ridiculously expensive. Mostly everyone walks or takes the Metro. Sometimes we take cabs, but not as often. It is a city, so it is not easy to find a parking space."

Q "Don't bring a car; it's not worth it. There are always taxi services and Metro subways that take you anywhere you need. You won't need a car until at least junior year, if ever. Plus, **in the city, it's expensive to maintain a car**."

Q "**You don't need a car at all**. Between the Metro and cabs, not to mention walking, having your own car is just not needed. From what I've noticed, parking gets a little hard to do and expensive."

Q "My suggestion is not to bring a car. You won't need it, and it will be a large expense. **Campus street parking is metered during the week**, and there are garages, but they charge a lot. I got by for four years without a car."

The College Prowler Take On...
Parking

There is no need to bring a car to GW. It becomes more of a hassle than a bonus to look for parking, pay for parking, and make sure your car does not get towed if you park illegally. There are several on-campus garages students can use, but they are all very expensive ($710 per month), and space is rather limited. Many off-campus apartment buildings have garages, too, but they can be equally expensive. It is also difficult to find a spot on the street when going out, day or night, in Georgetown, Dupont Circle, Adams Morgan, and other crowded areas.

The majority of GW students do not have cars—they see no need to spend the extra money on something they will rarely use. Yes, a car is convenient for traveling home, making it cheaper than flying or taking a train. But finding parking and paying for it is so difficult that most students prefer to use public transportation when going home, visiting a friend at another school, or traveling around DC. Students with cars will find their services in high demand when their friends—and people they hardly know, for that matter—want to take a trip to IHOP, located in Virginia.

The College Prowler® Grade on

A high grade in this section indicates that parking is both available and affordable, and that parking enforcement isn't overly severe.

Transportation

The Lowdown On...
Transportation

Ways to Get Around Town:

On Campus

4-RIDE escort service,
7 p.m.– 6 a.m. daily,
(202) 994-RIDE

Colonial Express Shuttle Bus,
7 p.m.–3 a.m. daily,
(202) 994-RIDE

Public Transportation

Washington Area
Metro Transit Authority:

The Metro (subway)
Monday–Thursday
5:30 a.m.–12 a.m., Friday 5:30
a.m.–3 a.m., Saturday 7 a.m.–
3 a.m., Sunday 7 a.m.–12 a.m.

The Foggy Bottom Metro
stop is located directly on
GW's campus, next to the
GW Hospital.

The Metrobus
24 hours a day, 7 days a week

→

(Public Transportation, continued)

Georgetown Shuttle Bus

Monday–Thursday 7 a.m.–midnight, Friday 7 a.m.–2 a.m., Saturday 8 a.m.–2 a.m., Sunday 8 a.m.–midnight

Buses leave every 10 minutes from the Foggy Bottom stop, located outside the Foggy Bottom Metro station

Taxi Cabs

Capitol Cab Co., (202) 546-2400

City Cab Co., (202) 829-4222

Diamond Cab Co., (202) 387-6200

Red Top Cab Co., (202) 328-3333

Yellow Cab Co., (202) 544-1212

Car Rentals

Alamo, local: (202) 363-3232; national: (800) 327-9633, www.alamo.com

Avis, local: (202) 467-6585; national: (800) 831-2847, www.avis.com

Enterprise, local: (202) 269-0300; national: (800) 736-8222, www.enterprise.com

Hertz, national: (800) 654-3131, www.hertz.com

Best Ways to Get Around Town

Walk

Georgetown Shuttle

Metro

Ways to Get Out of Town:

Airlines Serving Washington

American Airlines, (800) 433-7300, www.americanairlines.com

Continental, (800) 523-3273, www.continental.com

Delta, (800) 221-1212, www.delta-air.com

Northwest, (800) 225-2525, www.nwa.com

Southwest, (800) 435-9792, www.southwest.com

United, (800) 241-6522, www.united.com

US Airways, (800) 428-4322, www.usairways.com

Airports

Ronald Regan National Airport, (703) 417-8000

How to Get There

Take the Super Shuttle, a blue van that comes right to your door. The trip takes about 20 minutes and costs $15 for individual riders plus $8 for each additional person. You can also take the Metro.

Washington Dulles
International Airport,
(703) 572-2700

How to Get There

Take the Super Shuttle. The
trip takes about 40 minutes
and costs $15 for individual
riders, plus $10 for each
additional person.

Baltimore Washington
International Airport,
(800) FLY-BWI

How to Get There

Take the Marc Train from Union
Station to the BWI Rail Station
and then take the free Super
Shuttle to your terminal. The
trip takes about 45minutes
total, and the train costs
$6 per person.

Amtrak

Amtrak service is available
in Union Station, about a
fifteen-minute cab or Metro
ride (on the Red Line) away.
For schedule information call
1-800-USA-RAIL or visit
www.amtrak.com.

Travel Agents

STA Travel, the Marvin Center,
(202) 994-7800

Students Speak Out On...
Transformation

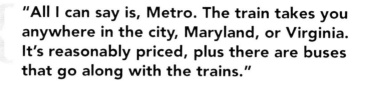

"All I can say is, Metro. The train takes you anywhere in the city, Maryland, or Virginia. It's reasonably priced, plus there are buses that go along with the trains."

"**The Metro takes you everywhere you could ever want to go** and even to places you wouldn't ever need to go—all this for a little more than a dollar. The Metro is also renowned for its cleanliness and efficiency."

"**Public transportation is really convenient**. Most of the time, you will use the Metro subway system. GW has its own stop. If the Metro doesn't take you there, the bus will."

"It's very convenient. There is a Metro system, and there is a bus system. Plus, **we are close to National Airport and Union Station**, where the Amtrak trains come in."

"The public transportation system in DC—particularly the Metro—is **modern, clean, safe, and convenient**."

"**The Metro is the way to go**, especially since cabs are pricey."

"There are tons of cabs and, of course, the Metro. And **you can walk almost everywhere**. There are also buses if you need to get places where the Metro doesn't go."

$\mathcal{Q}$ "If you take a cab, know your zones because, guaranteed, **they'll rip you off**."

$\mathcal{Q}$ "**Walking is easiest** and gets you around."

The College Prowler Take On...
Transportation

With a Metro stop and bus stops on campus, public transportation is conveniently located. It is also easy to use and will take students almost anywhere they want to go. The Metro, Washington's subway system, is easy to figure out and cheap—a little more than a dollar will get you to most places in and around the District. The Georgetown Shuttle Bus picks students up right outside the Metro station and takes them to several spots in Georgetown for only $1. The only bad part about DC transportation is the taxi system. Cab drivers dole out fares according to zones, rather than meters, so trips end up being quite expensive. Cab rides usually cost around $6 or $7, depending on time of day. Plus, riders are charged $1.50 for each additional person in the car.

Union Station provides Amtrak service to several major cities and is close to campus. Riders can also get 15 percent off their fare by using a Student Advantage Card, a discount card and a staple for GW students. GW also offers a bus to Philadelphia and New York during the holidays for a reasonable price. Services Zipcar and Flexcar, which offer students cars for under $10 per hour, are great for nighttime runs to the grocery store or day trips to local sites such as Old Town Alexandria or Baltimore. The bus system is a little tougher to figure out than the subway system, but it is still manageable. The city is relatively small, so even if a student gets on the wrong bus or train, he can find his way home.

The College Prowler® Grade on

A high grade for Transportation indicates that campus buses, public buses, cabs, and rental cars are readily-available and affordable. Other determining factors include proximity to an airport and the necessity of transportation.

Weather

The Lowdown On...
Weather

Average Temperature:

Fall: 69 °F
Winter: 42 °F
Spring: 66 °F
Summer: 88 °F

Average Precipitation:

Fall: 3.01 in.
Winter: 3.04 in.
Spring: 3.33 in.
Summer: 3.89 in.

Students Speak Out On...
Weather

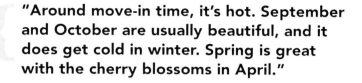

"Around move-in time, it's hot. September and October are usually beautiful, and it does get cold in winter. Spring is great with the cherry blossoms in April."

"I love DC in the spring and fall. The weather is tough to beat. If you enjoy the changing seasons, you'll like DC. **It gets really cold in the winter** and really hot in the summer, but in between, it's just perfect."

"The weather is cold in winters, hot in summers, and beautiful in the short springs and falls. **It does rain a lot, in my opinion.**"

"The weather is pretty hot up until December. **The humidity in DC is ridiculous.** A lot of my West Coast friends had to adjust to the humidity."

"You never know in DC. One day it can be in the 50s and the next it's in the nineties. **It's extremely unpredictable from one day to the next.**"

"For the most part, the weather is enjoyable. **It's not too cold in the winter, and usually fall starts in later October.** It can get very hot in the spring and early fall."

"**The weather is pretty mild**, though it can be a bit humid in the very beginning and end of the school year."

Q "DC is unpredictable. It lies between northern and southern climates, so you tend to feel both. There was more rain than I expected, and it gets very humid in the spring/early summer. **The wind chill can make the winters seem worse than they are**. They say snow is rare in DC, but we had two snow days last year. You just never know what to expect."

The College Prowler Take On...
Weather

DC has a pretty regular four-season climate. When students arrive in late August, it is still very hot and muggy, and the weather stays warm until late fall when the cold front moves in. Winters are pretty cold—bring a wool or down coat, sweaters, long pants, and boots. In the fall and spring, students wear jeans, Capri pants, and light jackets. But get ready for some hot, hot summers when planning to stay in DC. The humidity and heat can be unbearable, so take a dip in the Hall on Virginia Avenue's rooftop pool or City Hall's pool to cool off, or hope your internship office is air-conditioned (don't worry, dorms are).

Bring a variety of clothing to GW—pants, shorts, T-shirts, long-sleeved shirts, sweaters, jackets, and coats; you'll need it all. And don't forget an umbrella—rain is pretty common in the District.

The College Prowler® Grade on

A high Weather grade designates that temperatures are mild and rarely reach extremes, that the campus tends to be sunny rather than rainy, and that weather is fairly consistent rather than unpredictable.

THE GEORGE WASHINGTON UNIVERSITY

Report Card Summary

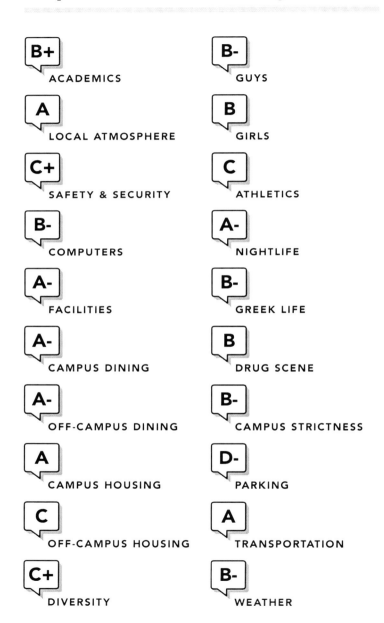

B+
ACADEMICS

A
LOCAL ATMOSPHERE

C+
SAFETY & SECURITY

B-
COMPUTERS

A-
FACILITIES

A-
CAMPUS DINING

A-
OFF-CAMPUS DINING

A
CAMPUS HOUSING

C
OFF-CAMPUS HOUSING

C+
DIVERSITY

B-
GUYS

B
GIRLS

C
ATHLETICS

A-
NIGHTLIFE

B-
GREEK LIFE

B
DRUG SCENE

B-
CAMPUS STRICTNESS

D-
PARKING

A
TRANSPORTATION

B-
WEATHER

Overall Experience

Students Speak Out On...
Overall Experience

"The administration is horrible, and it is a complete joke to get anything done with financial aid, but the professors are wonderful, and there is so much to do and see in the city."

Q "I would like to prepare freshmen for the fact that there are going to be lots of people that suck. **There are lots of snobby, rich girls from New York and New Jersey**. But on the other hand, I have met some of the coolest people ever. You really need to find your niche at GW, and once you do, things are all good. There are some great professors, and living in the city gives you the opportunity to get some really great internships while you are an undergrad."

Q "GW was exactly the school I wanted to go to. After high school, I was ready for change and ready to go out to the real world. To this day, I still know that coming to GW was probably one of the best decisions I have ever made. DC is probably one of my favorite cities in the country, and since going to GW, I have made some of the best friends I have ever known. I also had the opportunity to study abroad, which I recommend to everyone. **GW truly is a school that encourages independence** and allows everyone their own path. The student body is so diverse that you'll always find people who are similar to you at GW. GW is a school that becomes what you make of it. Everyone who goes there has a different experience. I would never change my decision to go here, and I'm glad I'm here."

Q "All I can say is that I had trouble deciding where to go to school. However, there's nothing bad I can say about GW. **I absolutely love it here**."

Q "I absolutely loved the past four years at GW. I just graduated and cannot think of a better place to have gone to school. Washington, DC was the most exciting and amazing city in which to attend college and live. The shopping, restaurants, bars, clubs, historical sites, and cultural things leave nothing to be desired. They are all top-notch and make going to GW that much better. Although **there is a lot of red tape at GW**, the overall experience you'll have here and all the positives of the school and the city far outweigh the negatives."

Q "**For the most part, I loved my experience at GW**. I made great friends, saw a lot of the city, and learned valuable lessons in my classes. I have no regrets about going to GW. You get twice the education here that any university can offer because it's right in the heart of DC, where all the action is taking place."

Q "It was hard for me to adjust to GW at first. Actually, it was really hard. It can be a very image-conscious place, and the urban location did grate on me. I even applied to transfer but ended up deciding to stay. I would not want to be anywhere else now, though. It is a school with a lot of very intelligent, open-minded, and generally cool people, and there is a lot to do. You will just have to **make an effort to seek out people who you like and** avoid those who are shallow and petty. If you work at it, GW can be a fantastic place, but it can also seem like a trap if you let things pile up."

The College Prowler Take On...
Overall Experience

Students at GW tend to complain a lot about the bureaucratic administration, pricey tuition, perhaps unnecessary new facilities, and excessive nickel-and-diming. However, most students stay at GW for four years—GW's retention rate is 92 percent. Many students are also upset about how GW compares academically to other schools, and that the science labs and facilities are run-down and old. GW students want the best and sometimes the University does not live up to their expectations.

Although GW provides students with a large variety of entertaining on-campus activities, students can also go off-campus and enjoy the city. The University's location in Washington makes most GW students' experiences worthwhile and interesting. GW would not be the same, or as wonderful, if it were not located in DC. The city adds life, variety, and uniqueness to the campus environment. Students have the opportunity to land internships while taking classes; to attend off-campus shows, productions, and sporting events; to dine at different restaurants; to bar- and club- hop; to explore museums; or to just relax for the day by the monuments or at the Waterfront. Washington is the perfect college town because it attracts young people from all over the country, gives students amazing opportunities, and is easy to manage. GW is a great place to be—most students are happy to spend their four years here.

The Inside Scoop

The Lowdown On...
The Inside Scoop

GW Slang

Know the slang, know the school. The following is a list of things you really need to know before coming to GW. The more of these words you know, the better off you'll be.

2000 Penn - GW's mall, located at 2000 Pennsylvania Ave. NW.

ABP - Au Bon Pain, the French bakery/cafe in 2000 Penn.

Big George/Little George - GW's two Colonials mascots.

Buyback - When you sell your books back at the end of the semester.

Club G - The Gelman Library during finals—everyone who is anyone is there.

CCAS - Columbian College of Arts and Sciences.

CF - Community Facilitator, similar to a Resident Adviser at other college campuses.

CI - Colonial Inauguration, GW's freshman orientation program.

Colonial Cash - GW's meal plan.

CRN - Course Registration Number, the five-digit number that identifies a course, used when you register.

➡

EMeRG - Emergency Medical Response Group, a 24-hour, student-employed medical service.

ESIA - Elliott School of International Affairs

Fall Fest and Spring Fling - Outdoor concerts/festivals sponsored by the student-run Program Board.

The Ghetto-vator - Thurston Hall's service elevator—it's broken down, but with 1,000 students sharing two regular elevators, sometimes it is the only way to go.

The *GW Hatchet* - The independent student newspaper.

GWorld - GW's ID card.

HOVA - Hall on Virginia Avenue.

Hippo - GW's unofficial mascot.

Hippodrome - Fifth floor of the Marvin Center, with bowling, billiards, and Big Burger.

J Street - GW's food court on the first floor of the Marvin Center.

Kogan Plaza - The outdoor area in the center of campus.

Manouch - GW's favorite hot dog vendor, comes out late at night by Tower Records.

MPD - Metropolitan Police Department.

PB - Program Board, GW's student programming organization.

Provo - Provisions Market, the grocery store in the Marvin Center.

SA - The Student Association, GW's student government.

SEAS - School of Engineering and Applied Science.

Sexiled - Getting kicked out of your room when your roommate is gettin' busy.

SJS - Student Judicial Services.

SJT - Stephen Joel Trachtenberg, University President.

SMPA - School of Media and Public Affairs.

STAR - Student Admissions Representative, a campus tour guide.

Student Advantage - Discount card accepted at several off-campus locations and by many public transportation companies.

UPD - University Police Department.

Things I Wish I Knew Before Coming to GW

- The majority of students are from the East Coast.

- Even if you avoid the "Freshman 15," you can still gain the "Sophomore 15" or "Junior 15."

- Freshmen do not really have to sign up for early or late classes—the University tells you this so everyone will get a certain number of classes at good times. But you don't have to, so don't do it.

- Try not to schedule a lot of morning classes because you will want to sleep late. Also, don't take Friday classes because Thursday is a party night. You may want to intern on Fridays.

- The GW mail and package facility is really slow and messes up a lot, so if you can, send your packages and mail to your off-campus work address (if you have one). GW's e-mail system also has its share of problems.

- Thurston Hall is the fun, party dorm. The Hall on Virginia Avenue is still fun but a little quieter. Don't live in any other freshman dorms.

Tips to Succeed at GW

- Research your professors before choosing your classes.

- Spend some time at the Gelman Library.

- Get to know professors well—they often have connections in the "real world" and can help you out with jobs and recommendations.

- Pursue what you love. GW has so many different clubs, organizations, and job opportunities that you're bound to find something that interests you.

- Stay for a summer at GW—you will have a lot of fun, plus there are great job opportunities available.

- Get an internship.

- Keep updated on campus news by reading the *Hatchet*. You can't complain about GW policies and procedures if you're not informed.

- Stay active—the Health and Wellness Center is great; there are some fun one-credit exercise classes. Intramural and club sports are also a great way to get involved.

- Explore DC and take advantage of the city.

- Work hard, but above all, enjoy yourself. This is the only time in your life when you'll be away from home, taking classes, and living with people your own age, unless you go to grad school. Going away to college is a unique opportunity, so make the most of it.

GW Urban Legends

- Each shoe on the shoe tree in front of the former Delta Tau Delta fraternity house represents a girl a brother has "de-virginized."

- Thurston Hall is one of the most sexually active dorms in the country.

- Touching the Hippo in front of Lisner Auditorium will bring you good luck.

- Sororities couldn't have houses until recently because an antiquated DC law considered them to be brothels.

School Spirit

Because GW athletics are not overwhelmingly popular, school spirit is definitely lacking. Although some students enjoy attending men's basketball games, GW's most popular sport, most rarely show up to cheer on the team.

Traditions

Commencement on the Ellipse

Unless there are severe weather conditions, GW students graduate on the Ellipse in front of the White House every year. Ending your four years at GW at this prestigious spot is beautiful and memorable.

Late-night trips to the monuments

When it's a quiet, warm night, students love hanging out at the monuments. Whether with a date (it's a really romantic spot) or a group of friends, nothing compares to staring at the reflecting pool from the top steps of the Lincoln Memorial at 2 a.m.

Midnight Breakfast

Each fall and spring during finals, the University hosts a

Midnight Breakfast at the Marvin Center. Students race to get in line for eggs, tater tots, muffins, and fruit. There are also games and activities throughout the Marvin Center to help students de-stress.

Spring Break
Whether partying on the beaches of Cancun or Mexico or backpacking around Europe, most GW students take advantage of spring break to get out of DC with their GW friends. There are several special student deals to places in and out of the country. The most popular spots are the Bahamas, Florida, Jamaica, and Mexico. Get ready for a week of drunken madness.

Mount Vernon Brunch
Waking up on a Saturday or Sunday morning, the last thing freshmen want to do is trek over to the Marvin Center for an Einstein Bros. bagel. But, surprisingly, students head to Mount Vernon, located a shuttle ride away, because the Mount Vernon campus' Ames Dining Hall has the best brunch on campus. With a swipe of your GWorld card, you can get cereal, eggs, muffins, pancakes, and more.

Finding a Job or Internship

The Lowdown On...
Finding a Job or Internship

There are plenty of jobs and internships available on and off campus, work study and non-work study. Almost all GW students will have at least one internship or job related to their field of study by the end of their four years in the District. Internships are a great way gateway to a long-term career.

Advice
The best ways to find out about internships is through professors, other students, and the Internet (*www.monster. com*, *www.wetfeet.com*, and a plethora of both general and major-specific sites). Another way to find out about internships is to call up local companies to ask if they are hiring. Peruse the Yellow Pages and start making phone calls. Although some companies do not advertise on large Web sites, they may still be looking for interns.

Career Center Resources & Services

Job fairs

Alumni Networking Connection

GW Job Trak

Resume critiques

Resource Room (with binders of job listings)

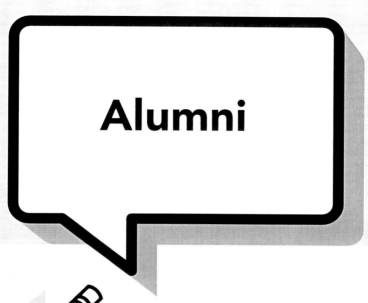

The Lowdown On...
Alumni

Web Site:
www.alumni.gwu.edu

Office:
1925 F St. NW
Phone: (202) 994-6435
Fax: (202) 994-8060

Services Available:

Alumni Admissions Program

Alumni can interview prospective students, host receptions at their homes, and represent GW at college fairs.

Auto/Home Insurance Program

Alumni qualify for a special group discount on auto, home, and renters insurance through Group Savings Plus from Liberty Mutual.

➔

Career Services
Several career and networking services are available.

Course Audit Program
Alumni can take certain GW courses for $100 per semester.

GWAA Credit Card Program
When alumni use the GW Alumni Association Platinum Plus MasterCard, a portion of every purchase goes to support alumni activities and services.

Message Forwarding
The Alumni House will forward messages to alumni's current mailing addresses. Alumni also receive an "@alumni.gwu.edu" forwarding e-mail address.

Medical Insurance Program
Alumni can purchase insurance through GW.

Major Alumni Events
The major event for alumni and families of current students is Colonials Weekend, which is somewhat like bigger schools' homecoming weekends. Alumni have the chance to attend events put on by various departments within the University, as well as see how GW has changed since they left.

Alumni Publications
GW Magazine

Did You Know?

Famous Alumni

Arnold "Red" Auerbach (BS '40, MA '41, DPS '93) - President and former coach, Boston Celtics

Abby Joseph Cohen (MA '76) - Managing Director, Goldman, Sachs & Co.

Kent Conrad (MBA '75) - U.S. Senator (North Dakota)

Michael Enzi (BBA '66) - U.S. Senator (Wyoming)

Daniel Inouye (JD '52) - U.S. Senator (Hawaii)

Edward Liddy (MBA '72) - Chairman, CEO and President, Allstate Corp.

Abe Pollin (BA '45) - Chairman, Washington Wizards and Washington Capitals

General Colin Powell (MBA '71) - Secretary of State

Harry Reid (JD '64) - U.S. Senator (Nevada)

John Snow (JD '67) - Secretary of the Treasury

Mark Warner (BA '77) - Governor of Virginia

Scott Wolf (BBA '88) - Actor

Student Organizations

612 Noise

2004 Strong Hall Council

Aatash

Active Minds

Afghan Student Organization

Agape Campus
Christian Fellowship

AGHAST

AIESEC

Aikido GWU

Alpha Chi Sigma,
Alpha Pi Chapter

Alpha Delta Pi Sorority

Alpha Epsilon Phi

Alpha Epsilon Pi

Alpha Iota Mu

Alpha Kappa Alpha
Sorority, Incorporated

Alpha Phi Fraternity

Alpha Phi Omega

American Studies
Student Organization

Amnesty International

APIA Organization Council

Arnold Air Society

Asian Baptist Student Koinonia

Association of Forensic Science
Students

Athletes in Action

The Ballroom Dance Society

Beer $ For Kerry

Best Buddies

Beta Alpha Psi Fraternity

BIAS-Black International Affairs
Society

Black Law Students Association

Black Student Union

BLAZEN

Books for Africa Student
Organization

Caribbean Student Association

Chinese Students and Scholars Association

Chronic Illness Action Network

Cigar Smokers Forum

Circle K

Citizens Commission to Protect the Truth

Club Softball

Club Tennis

Coalition for a Sustainable GW

The College WISH List

Colonial Army

Colonials for Kerry

Comparative Empires Working Group

Conflict Resolution Forum

Conservative Student Union

Cosponsorship Organization

The *Daily Colonial*

Dance Performance Project

Delta Gamma Fraternity

Delta Sigma Pi

Doctoral Students Association

East Coast Asian American Student Union

Educational Technology and Leadership Student Orga

Emergency Medical Response Group (EMeRG)

Engineers Without Borders

Epsilon Sigma Alpha

ESIA Graduate Student Forum

Fondue and Foreign Policy Club

Foundation of International Medical Relief for Chi

Generic Theatre Company

George Washington Bujinkan Club

George Washington University Collegiate Chess League

The George Washington University Dance Dance Revol

George Washington University Gamers Society

The George Washington University Model Congress

The George Washington University Toastmasters Club

The George Washington University X-Box Club

German Club

Global Ethics Society

Global Leadership Interlink-GW

Global Perspectives Living and Learning Community

GW ACLU

GW Boot Camp for Life

GW Boxing Club

GW Campaign to End the Death Penalty

GW Cherry Tree

GW College Republicans

GW Fencing

GW Gaming League

GW Japanese Student Society

GW Junior Class Council

GW Khiladi

GW MBA Sailing Club

GW NOW

The GW Pitches

GW Pre Optometry Club

GW Senior Education

GW Sophomore Class Council

GW Sports Marketing Association

GW Students for Fair Trade

GW Students Taking Action Now: Darfur (STAND)

GW Taekwon-Do

GW Transfers

The GW Vibes

GW Wine Institute 'N' Organization

GW Women's Club Soccer

GW-SPAN

GW-TV.com

GWU Chinese Bible Study

GWU Dodgeball League

GWU Habitat for Humanity

GWU Volleyball club

Health Services Management and Leadership Student

Healthy Lifestyles Living and Learning Community

History Grad Student Forum

Holy Land Christian College Community

HOVA Hall Council

Human and Organizational Studies (HOS) Student Association

The Human Service Student Organization

Independent Students Alliance

Indian Students' Association

INQUIRY

The Institute for Biomedical Sciences Graduate Students

International Alternative Spring Break Association

International College Film Organization

International Education Association

International MBA Association (IMBAA)

International Student Christian Association

InterVarsity Christian Fellowship

Intervarsity Graduate Christian Fellowship

Iota Nu Delta

Iranian Cultural Society

Ivory Tower Residence Hall Association

The J.O.S.H. Project

The Jackie Robinson Society

Japanese Student Association

Jenny's Memorial Fund

Jewish Student Association

JKA Karate Club of GWU

Kappa Alpha Psi

Kappa Sigma Fraternity, Alpha-Eta Chapter

Kosmos Hellenic Club

La Unidad Latina, Lambda Upsilon Lambda Fraternity

Lafayette Residence Hall Executive Board

Latinas Promoviendo Comunidad/Lambda Pi Chi Sorority

Latter-day Saint Student Association

The Lawn Sports And Barbecue Club

LIFELINE

Liquid Arts

Mabel Thurston Residence Hall Association

Majority Productions

Master of Public Administration Association

Med School Class of 2008 Class Council

Medical Ethics Student Association

Men's Ultimate Frisbee

Minority Association of Pre-Health Students

Minority Business Student Association

Mock Trial

Mortar and Pestle Literary Magazine

Multicultural Cooking Club

Muslim Students' Association

The National Society of Collegiate Scholars (NSCS)

Off the Sound Post

Omicron Delta Kappa

Organization for the Preservation of Peace Studies

Organization Of African Students

Organization of Latino American Students

The Out Crowd

Outdoor Adventure

Outside the Box

The Pakistani Student Association

The Panhellenic Association

Parliamentary Debate Society

Pelham Hall Council

Phi Eta Sigma

Phi Kappa Psi

Phi Sigma Kappa

Pi Delta Psi Fraternity, Inc.

Pi Kappa Alpha

Pi Kappa Phi

Politics And Media Living and Learning Community

The Pre-Law Society

Project HEALTH

Psychology Graduate Student Forum (PGSF)

Public Policy Student Association

Puerto Rico Statehood Society

RAISE (Raising Awareness Involving Survivor Empowe

Real Estate Investment & Development Organization

Recycling Club

Republican Jewish Coalition GW Chapter

Republocrats

Residence Hall Association

Rhythm Living and Learning Community

The Rock Christian Fellowship

Run 5 - 4 Life

S.T.A.N.D. (Students Taking Action Not Drugs)

Serve DC

Shiluv

Sigma Alpha Lambda - GWU Chapter

Sigma Delta Tau

Sigma Nu Fraternity

Sigma Phi Epsilon

Sigma Psi Zeta

Sikh Students' Association

The Sirens

The Society of Exercise Science Students

Somers Residence Hall Council

Sons of Pitch

South Asian Society

Sports and Recreation

Student Athlete
Advisory Council

Student Bar Association

Student design Society

Student Global
AIDS Campaign

Student Theatre Council

Students Defending
Democracy

Students for Bush

Students for Organ Donation

Tau Beta Pi

Tau Kappa Epsilon

The George Washington Art
Therapy Student Association

Theta Tau Fraternity - Gamma
Beta Chapter

Turkish Student Association

Unite for Sight

United States Campaign
for Burma

Vietnamese Student
Association

Voices of Inspiration

W Stands for Women

Washington Free Collaboration

Women On the Move! The GW
YPWC Society

Women's Ultimate
Frisbee Team

Word Up! Bible Study

Working Undergrads

WRGW

Yad B'Yad (Hand In Hand)

Yad Echad

Yesteryear Living and
Learning Community

Young Asian Americans for
Kerry Edwards

Young Women of Color-
DC Chapter

Note:

Since organizations are
constantly re-registering their
statuses with GW, the most
up-to-date information can be
found online at:
http://studentorgs.gwu.edu
and by clicking on "Directory
of Student Orgs."

The Best & Worst

The Ten **BEST** Things About GW

1	Meeting cool people
2	Located in Washington, DC
3	Internship opportunities
4	College campus feel, in the middle of the city
5	Top-of-the-line facilities and dorms
6	Colonial Cash meal plan
7	Great bars, clubs, and restaurants nearby
8	Private bathrooms in most dorm rooms
9	Hanging out on Kogan Plaza or by the Waterfront on a sunny day
10	Going to the monuments at night

The Ten **WORST** Things About GW

1 High tuition that keeps increasing

2 Lack of school spirit

3 Expensive housing

4 Study abroad options limited to about 200 GW-affiliated programs rather than thousands of unaffiliated programs

5 No football team

6 University and Metropolitan Police's strictness concerning underage drinking

7 Slow 4-RIDE service

8 The centralized package facility—having to pick packages up instead of having them delivered to dorms

9 Red tape and bureaucratic procedures

10 University's strict policies concerning fraternities and sororities, although GW claims to want a larger Greek community

Visiting

The Lowdown On...
Visiting

Hotel Information:

Doubletree Guest Suites
801 New Hampshire Ave. NW,
Foggy Bottom
(202) 785-2000
www.washingtondcsuites
.doubletree.com
Price Range: $109–$279

Embassy Suites
1250 22nd St. NW,
Foggy Bottom
(202) 857-3388
www.embassysuites.com
Price Range: $99–$300

Georgetown Suites
1111 30th St. NW,
Georgetown
(202) 298-7800
www.georgetownsuites.com
Price Range: $135–$165

➔

One Washington Circle
1 Washington Circle NW,
Foggy Bottom
(202) 872-1680
www.onewashhotel.com
Price Range: $175–$345

State Plaza
2117 E St. NW,
Foggy Bottom
(202) 861-8200
www.washingtonplaza.com/sp/
Price Range: $85–$195

Swissotel Watergate
2650 Virginia Ave. NW,
Foggy Bottom
(202) 965-2300
www.swissotel.com
Price Range: $149–$250

Westin Hotel
2350 M St. NW,
Foggy Bottom
(202) 429-0100
www.westin.com
Price Range: $189–$560

Campus Tours

Tours are available Monday–Friday starting at 11 a.m. A final tour of Mount Vernon begins at 4:45 p.m., and Saturday, it begins at 11 a.m. with a final tour of Mount Vernon beginning at 3:45 p.m. Information sessions precede campus tours at 10 a.m. Monday-Saturday and last for an hour.

Take a Campus Virtual Tour

http://gwired.gwu.edu/adm/visit/res_frame.html

Overnight Visits

Contact the Student Network Admissions Program at (202) 994-0432 or gwstar@gwu.edu.

To Schedule a Group Information Session or Interview

Call the GW Visitor Center at (202) 994-6602.

Directions to Campus

Driving from the North

- Take Interstate 95 South to Interstate 495 (Capital Beltway) toward Silver Spring/Northern Virginia.
- Take exit 33, heading south on Connecticut Avenue for about nine miles. Turn right onto Florida Avenue (just past the Washington Hilton) and turn left immediately onto 21st Street.
- Turn right on I Street. The visitor entrance to the parking garage is on the left between 22nd and 23rd streets.

Driving from the South

- Take Interstate 95 to Interstate 395 Arlington Memorial Bridge exit.
- Cross the bridge and bear left at the Lincoln Memorial. Turn left onto 23rd Street and follow directions as given from West.

Driving from the Northwest

- Take Interstate 270 to Interstate 495 (Capital Beltway) toward Silver Spring.
- Take exit 33, heading south on Connecticut Avenue for about nine miles. Follow directions as given from North.

Driving from the West

- Interstate 66 and Route 50 both connect with the Theodore Roosevelt Bridge.
- Cross the bridge and exit left at E Street, then again at Virginia Avenue. Bear left, following signs for 23rd Street.
- Turn right on 23rd Street and continue a few blocks to campus.
- Turn right on I Street. The visitor entrance to the parking garage is on your right between 22nd and 23rd streets.

Words to Know

Academic Probation – A suspension imposed on a student if he or she fails to keep up with the school's minimum academic requirements. Those unable to improve their grades after receiving this warning can face dismissal.

Beer Pong / Beirut – A drinking game involving cups of beer arranged in a pyramid shape on each side of a table. The goal is to get a ping pong ball into one of the opponent's cups by throwing the ball or hitting it with a paddle. If the ball lands in a cup, the opponent is required to drink the beer.

Bid – An invitation from a fraternity or sorority to 'pledge' (join) that specific house.

Blue-Light Phone – Brightly-colored phone posts with a blue light bulb on top. These phones exist for security purposes and are located at various outside locations around most campuses. In an emergency, a student can pick up one of these phones (free of charge) to connect with campus police or a security escort.

Campus Police – Police who are specifically assigned to a given institution. Campus police are typically not regular city officers; they are employed by the university in a full-time capacity.

Club Sports – A level of sports that falls somewhere between varsity and intramural. If a student is unable to commit to a varsity team but has a lot of passion for athletics, a club sport could be a better, less intense option. Even less demanding, intramural (IM) sports often involve no traveling and considerably less time.

Cocaine – An illegal drug. Also known as "coke" or "blow," cocaine often resembles a white crystalline or powdery substance. It is highly addictive and dangerous.

Common Application – An application with which students can apply to multiple schools.

Course Registration – The period of official class selection for the upcoming quarter or semester. Prior to registration, it is best to prepare several back-up courses in case a particular class becomes full. If a course is full, students can place themselves on the waitlist, although this still does not guarantee entry.

Division Athletics – Athletic classifications range from Division I to Division III. Division IA is the most competitive, while Division III is considered to be the least competitive.

Dorm – A dorm (or dormitory) is an on-campus housing facility. Dorms can provide a range of options from suite-style rooms to more communal options that include shared bathrooms. Most first-year students live in dorms. Some upperclassmen who wish to stay on campus also choose this option.

Early Action – An application option with which a student can apply to a school and receive an early acceptance response without a binding commitment. This system is becoming less and less available.

Early Decision – An application option that students should use only if they are certain they plan to attend the school in question. If a student applies using the early decision option and is admitted, he or she is required and bound to attend that university. Admission rates are usually higher among students who apply through early decision, as the student is clearly indicating that the school is his or her first choice.

Ecstasy – An illegal drug. Also known as "E" or "X," ecstasy looks like a pill and most resembles an aspirin. Considered a party drug, ecstasy is very dangerous and can be deadly.

Ethernet – An extremely fast Internet connection available in most university-owned residence halls. To use an Ethernet connection properly, a student will need a network card and cable for his or her computer.

Fake ID – A counterfeit identification card that contains false information. Most commonly, students get fake IDs with altered birthdates so that they appear to be older than 21 (and therefore of legal drinking age). Even though it is illegal, many college students have fake IDs in hopes of purchasing alcohol or getting into bars.

Frosh – Slang for "freshman" or "freshmen."

Hazing – Initiation rituals administered by some fraternities or sororities as part of the pledging process. Many universities have outlawed hazing due to its degrading and sometimes dangerous nature.

Intramurals (IMs) – A popular, and usually free, sport league in which students create teams and compete against one another. These sports vary in competitiveness and can include a range of activities—everything from billiards to water polo. IM sports are a great way to meet people with similar interests.

Keg – Officially called a half-barrel, a keg contains roughly 200 12-ounce servings of beer.

LSD – An illegal drug. Also known as acid, this hallucinogenic drug most commonly resembles a tab of paper.

Marijuana – An illegal drug. Also known as weed or pot; along with alcohol, marijuana is one of the most commonly-found drugs on campuses across the country.

Major –The focal point of a student's college studies; a specific topic that is studied for a degree. Examples of majors include physics, English, history, computer science, economics, business, and music. Many students decide on a specific major before arriving on campus, while others are simply "undecided" until delcaring a major. Those who are extremely interested in two areas can also choose to double major.

Meal Block – The equivalent of one meal. Students on a meal plan usually receive a fixed number of meals per week. Each meal, or "block," can be redeemed at the school's dining facilities in place of cash. Often, a student's weekly allotment of meal blocks will be forfeited if not used.

Minor – An additional focal point in a student's education. Often serving as a complement or addition to a student's main area of focus, a minor has fewer requirements and prerequisites to fulfill than a major. Minors are not required for graduation from most schools; however some students who want to explore many different interests choose to pursue both a major and a minor.

Mushrooms – An illegal drug. Also known as "'shrooms," this drug resembles regular mushrooms but is extremely hallucinogenic.

Off-Campus Housing – Housing from a particular landlord or rental group that is not affiliated with the university. Depending on the college, off-campus housing can range from extremely popular to non-existent. Students who choose to live off campus are typically given more freedom, but they also have to deal with possible subletting scenarios, furniture, bills, and other issues. In addition to these factors, rental prices and distance often affect a student's decision to move off campus.

Office Hours – Time that teachers set aside for students who have questions about coursework. Office hours are a good forum for students to go over any problems and to show interest in the subject material.

Pledging – The early phase of joining a fraternity or sorority, pledging takes place after a student has gone through rush and received a bid. Pledging usually lasts between one and two semesters. Once the pledging period is complete and a particular student has done everything that is required to become a member, that student is considered a brother or sister. If a fraternity or a sorority would decide to "haze" a group of students, this initiation would take place during the pledging period.

Private Institution – A school that does not use tax revenue to subsidize education costs. Private schools typically cost more than public schools and are usually smaller.

Prof – Slang for "professor."

Public Institution – A school that uses tax revenue to subsidize education costs. Public schools are often a good value for in-state residents and tend to be larger than most private colleges.

Quarter System (or Trimester System) – A type of academic calendar system. In this setup, students take classes for three academic periods. The first quarter usually starts in late September or early October and concludes right before Christmas. The second quarter usually starts around early to mid–January and finishes up around March or April. The last academic quarter, or "third quarter," usually starts in late March or early April and finishes up in late May or Mid-June. The fourth quarter is summer. The major difference between the quarter system and semester system is that students take more, less comprehensive courses under the quarter calendar.

RA (Resident Assistant) – A student leader who is assigned to a particular floor in a dormitory in order to help to the other students who live there. An RA's duties include ensuring student safety and providing assistance wherever possible.

Recitation – An extension of a specific course; a review session. Some classes, particularly large lectures, are supplemented with mandatory recitation sessions that provide a relatively personal class setting.

Rolling Admissions – A form of admissions. Most commonly found at public institutions, schools with this type of policy continue to accept students throughout the year until their class sizes are met. For example, some schools begin accepting students as early as December and will continue to do so until April or May.

Room and Board – This figure is typically the combined cost of a university-owned room and a meal plan.

Room Draw/Housing Lottery – A common way to pick on-campus room assignments for the following year. If a student decides to remain in university-owned housing, he or she is assigned a unique number that, along with seniority, is used to determine his or her housing for the next year.

Rush – The period in which students can meet the brothers and sisters of a particular chapter and find out if a given fraternity or sorority is right for them. Rushing a fraternity or a sorority is not a requirement at any school. The goal of rush is to give students who are serious about pledging a feel for what to expect.

Semester System – The most common type of academic calendar system at college campuses. This setup typically includes two semesters in a given school year. The fall semester starts around the end of August or early September and concludes before winter vacation. The spring semester usually starts in mid-January and ends in late April or May.

Student Center/Rec Center/Student Union – A common area on campus that often contains study areas, recreation facilities, and eateries. This building is often a good place to meet up with fellow students; depending on the school, the student center can have a huge role or a non-existent role in campus life.

Student ID – A university-issued photo ID that serves as a student's key to school-related functions. Some schools require students to show these cards in order to get into dorms, libraries, cafeterias, and other facilities. In addition to storing meal plan information, in some cases, a student ID can actually work as a debit card and allow students to purchase things from bookstores or local shops.

Suite – A type of dorm room. Unlike dorms that feature communal bathrooms shared by the entire floor, suites offer bathrooms shared only among the suite. Suite-style dorm rooms can house anywhere from two to ten students.

TA (Teacher's Assistant) – An undergraduate or grad student who helps in some manner with a specific course. In some cases, a TA will teach a class, assist a professor, grade assignments, or conduct office hours.

Undergraduate – A student in the process of studying for his or her bachelor's degree.

ABOUT THE AUTHOR

Julie Gordon graduated from GW with a major in journalism and a minor in English. A Livingston, New Jersey native, Julie was excited to have had the chance to write a book about something she loves so much—GW. On campus, Julie was news managing editor of the century-old *GW Hatchet*, the University's independent student newspaper, during her senior year. She was also University news editor her junior year, and a reporter and staff writer her sophomore year. Julie was an editorial intern at *USA Today* in summer 2003, and covered the shooting at City Hall in New York, IMG founder Mark McCormack's memorial service, the New York smoking ban, and a bunch of literary and entertainment news, among other stories. Julie also interned in *YM* magazine's entertainment department in summer 2002. Julie is pursuing a career in journalism or public relations.

Julie was also involved in theater at GW. She co-founded a student-run theater company, 14th Grade Players, her sophomore year. She made her directorial debut in April 2002 with Barbara Lebow's *A Shayna Maidel*. Julie produced *Deathtrap*, by Ira Levin, in fall 2002, and served as public relations chair for the group in the 2003-04 academic year. Julie performed in two plays at GW—*The Crucible*, as Betty, and *Who Made Robert DeNiro King of America?*, as Samantha. She is also a member of the Screen Actors Guild.

Julie could not have written this book about GW if she had not met such wonderful people while attending school. Julia offers the following thanks:

"To Stefanie for being a wonderful roommate and friend for the past four years. Adina—we've had great times and have shared so much. My other friends and Hatcheteers—you're all great and have made my time at GW worthwhile. To the non-G-dubbers: Tracy, Liza, and Lauren—your friendships are so special to me. Mom and Dad—thank you for encouraging me to come to GW and pursue my writing. I love you. Emily—I wish we were in school together. I love you so much and know you'll do great in college. To those either looking at or attending GW, my time in the District has been wonderful, and I can't imagine being anywhere else."

E-mails may be sent to juliegordon@collegeprowler.com with any questions.

The College Prowler
Big Book of Colleges

Having Trouble Narrowing Down Your Choices?
Try Going Bigger!

BIG BOOK OF COLLEGES '08
7¼" X 10", 1106 Pages Paperback
$29.95 Retail
1-4274-0001-6

Choosing the perfect school can be an overwhelming challenge. Luckily, our *Big Book of Colleges* makes that task a little less daunting. We've packed it with overviews of our full library of single-school guides— nearly 250 of the nation's top schools—giving you some much-needed perspective on your search.

College Prowler on the Web

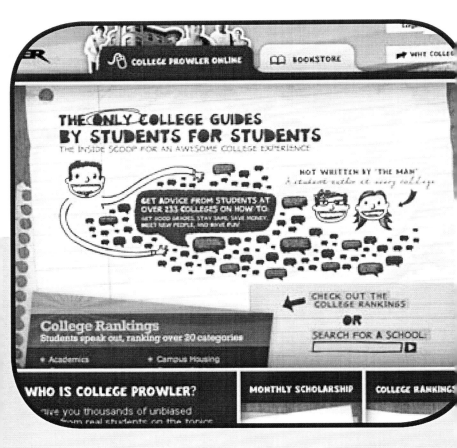

Craving some electronic interaction? Check out the new and improved **CollegeProwler.com**! We've included the COMPLETE contents of all 250 of our single-school guides on the Web—and you can gain access to all of them for just $39.95 per year!

Not only that, but non-subscribers can still view and compare our grades for each school, order books at our online bookstore, or enter our monthly scholarship contest. Don't get left in the dark when making your college decision. Let College Prowler be your guide!

Get the Hookup!

College Prowler Hookup gives you a peek behind the scenes

The Hookup is our new blog designed to hook you up with great information, funny videos, cool contests, awesome scholarship opportunities, and honest insight into who we are and what we're all about.

Check us out at *www.collegeprowlerhookup.com*

Need Help Paying For School?

Apply for our scholarship!

College Prowler awards thousands of dollars a year to students who compose the best essays. E-mail scholarship@collegeprowler.com for more information, or call 1-800-290-2682.

Apply now at ***www.collegeprowler.com***

Tell Us What Life Is Really Like at Your School!

Have you ever wanted to let people know what your college is really like? Now's your chance to help millions of high school students choose the right college.

Let your voice be heard.

Check out **www.collegeprowler.com** for more info!

Need More Help?

Do you have more questions about this school? Can't find a certain statistic? College Prowler is here to help. We are the best source of college information out there. We have a network of thousands of students who can get the latest information on any school to you ASAP. E-mail us at info@collegeprowler.com with your college-related questions.

E-Mail Us Your College-Related Questions!

Check out *www.collegeprowler.com* for more details.
1-800-290-2682

Write For Us!
Get published! Voice your opinion.

Writing a College Prowler guidebook is both fun and rewarding; our open-ended format allows your own creativity free reign. Our writers have been featured in national newspapers and have seen their names in bookstores across the country. Now is your chance to break into the publishing industry with one of the country's fastest-growing publishers!

Apply now at **www.collegeprowler.com**

Contact editor@collegeprowler.com or
call 1-800-290-2682 for more details.

Pros and Cons

Still can't figure out if this is the right school for you?
You've already read through this in-depth guide; why not
list the pros and cons? It will really help with narrowing down
your decision and determining whether or not
this school is right for you.

Pros	Cons
....	....
....	....
....	....
....	....
....	....
....	....
....	....
....	....
....	....
....	....
....	....
....	....
....	....
....	....

Pros and Cons

Still can't figure out if this is the right school for you?
You've already read through this in-depth guide; why not
list the pros and cons? It will really help with narrowing down
your decision and determining whether or not
this school is right for you.

Pros	Cons
....	....
....	....
....	....
....	....
....	....
....	....
....	....
....	....
....	....
....	....
....	....
....	....
....	....

Notes

....

....

....

....

....

....

....

....

....

....

....

....

....

Notes

....

....

....

....

....

....

....

....

....

....

....

....

....

Notes

....

....

....

....

....

....

....

....

....

....

....

....

....

Notes

....

....

....

....

....

....

....

....

....

....

....

....

....

Albion College
Alfred University
Allegheny College
American University
Amherst College
Arizona State University
Auburn University
Babson College
Ball State University
Bard College
Barnard College
Bates College
Baylor University
Beloit College
Bentley College
Binghamton University
Birmingham Southern College
Boston College
Boston University
Bowdoin College
Brandeis University
Brigham Young University
Brown University
Bryn Mawr College
Bucknell University
Cal Poly
Cal Poly Pomona
Cal State Northridge
Cal State Sacramento
Caltech
Carleton College
Carnegie Mellon University
Case Western Reserve
Centenary College of Louisiana
Centre College
Claremont McKenna College
Clark Atlanta University
Clark University
Clemson University
Colby College
Colgate University
College of Charleston
College of the Holy Cross
College of William & Mary
College of Wooster
Colorado College
Columbia University
Connecticut College
Cornell University
Creighton University
CUNY Hunters College
Dartmouth College
Davidson College
Denison University
DePauw University
Dickinson College
Drexel University
Duke University
Duquesne University
Earlham College
East Carolina University
Elon University
Emerson College
Emory University
FIT
Florida State University
Fordham University

Franklin & Marshall College
Furman University
Geneva College
George Washington University
Georgetown University
Georgia Tech
Gettysburg College
Gonzaga University
Goucher College
Grinnell College
Grove City College
Guilford College
Gustavus Adolphus College
Hamilton College
Hampshire College
Hampton University
Hanover College
Harvard University
Harvey Mudd College
Haverford College
Hofstra University
Hollins University
Howard University
Idaho State University
Illinois State University
Illinois Wesleyan University
Indiana University
Iowa State University
Ithaca College
IUPUI
James Madison University
Johns Hopkins University
Juniata College
Kansas State
Kent State University
Kenyon College
Lafayette College
LaRoche College
Lawrence University
Lehigh University
Lewis & Clark College
Louisiana State University
Loyola College in Maryland
Loyola Marymount University
Loyola University Chicago
Loyola University New Orleans
Macalester College
Marlboro College
Marquette University
McGill University
Miami University of Ohio
Michigan State University
Middle Tennessee State
Middlebury College
Millsaps College
MIT
Montana State University
Mount Holyoke College
Muhlenberg College
New York University
North Carolina State
Northeastern University
Northern Arizona University
Northern Illinois University
Northwestern University
Oberlin College
Occidental College

Ohio State University
Ohio University
Ohio Wesleyan University
Old Dominion University
Penn State University
Pepperdine University
Pitzer College
Pomona College
Princeton University
Providence College
Purdue University
Reed College
Rensselaer Polytechnic Institute
Rhode Island School of Design
Rhodes College
Rice University
Rochester Institute of Technology
Rollins College
Rutgers University
San Diego State University
Santa Clara University
Sarah Lawrence College
Scripps College
Seattle University
Seton Hall University
Simmons College
Skidmore College
Slippery Rock
Smith College
Southern Methodist University
Southwestern University
Spelman College
St. Joseph's University Philladelphia
St. John's University
St. Louis University
St. Olaf College
Stanford University
Stetson University
Stony Brook University
Susquhanna University
Swarthmore College
Syracuse University
Temple University
Tennessee State University
Texas A & M University
Texas Christian University
Towson University
Trinity College Connecticut
Trinity University Texas
Truman State
Tufts University
Tulane University
UC Berkeley
UC Davis
UC Irvine
UC Riverside
UC San Diego
UC Santa Barbara
UC Santa Cruz
UCLA
Union College
University at Albany
University at Buffalo
University of Alabama
University of Arizona
University of Central Florida
University of Chicago

University of Colorado
University of Connecticut
University of Delaware
University of Denver
University of Florida
University of Georgia
University of Illinois
University of Iowa
University of Kansas
University of Kentucky
University of Maine
University of Maryland
University of Massachusetts
University of Miami
University of Michigan
University of Minnesota
University of Mississippi
University of Missouri
University of Nebraska
University of New Hampshire
University of North Carolina
University of Notre Dame
University of Oklahoma
University of Oregon
University of Pennsylvania
University of Pittsburgh
University of Puget Sound
University of Rhode Island
University of Richmond
University of Rochester
University of San Diego
University of San Francisco
University of South Carolina
University of South Dakota
University of South Florida
University of Southern California
University of Tennessee
University of Texas
University of Utah
University of Vermont
University of Virginia
University of Washington
University of Wisconsin
UNLV
Ursinus College
Valparaiso University
Vanderbilt University
Vassar College
Villanova University
Virginia Tech
Wake Forest University
Warren Wilson College
Washington and Lee University
Washington University in St. Louis
Wellesley College
Wesleyan University
West Point
West Virginia University
Wheaton College IL
Wheaton College MA
Whitman College
Wilkes University
Williams College
Xavier University
Yale University